Silent Echoes

A True Story

Silent Echoes

A True Story

Amita Malhotra
(With a foreword by Shiv Khera)

NEW DAWN PRESS, INC.
UK • USA • INDIA

NEW DAWN PRESS GROUP
Published by New Dawn Press Group
New Dawn Press, Inc., 244 South Randall Rd # 90, Elgin, IL 60123
e-mail: sales@newdawnpress.com

New Dawn Press, 2 Tintern Close, Slough, Berkshire, SL1-2TB, UK
e-mail: ndpuk@newdawnpress.com

New Dawn Press (An Imprint of Sterling Publishers (P) Ltd.)
A-59, Okhla Industrial Area, Phase-II, New Delhi-110020
e-mail: info@sterlingpublishers.com
www.sterlingpublishers.com

Silent Echoes
©2005, Amita Malhotra
ISBN 1 84557 281 5

PRINTED IN INDIA

Dedication

*To my father, who always inspired me
and encouraged my creativity.
May he rest in peace.*

Disclaimer

In this book, the author Amita Malhotra, has narrated the true story of her personal friend, whose identity she has not disclosed to the publishers, in order to protect her privacy. Therefore, the incidents related in the story have not been verified by the publishers. The publishers assume NO responsibility for any errors or omissions. Neither is any liability assumed for damages resulting for the use of the story contained herein.

The publishers specifically disclaim any liability, loss or risk, whatsoever, personal, or otherwise, which is incurred as a consequence, directly, or indirectly of the use and application of any of the contents of this book.

The book is sold with the understanding that the publishers are not engaged in rendering legal, accounting, or other professional service.

Any publisher disputes that may arise in this matter are to be settled within the jurisdiction of courts in New Delhi only.

Although Prerna's story is true, the names of the characters have been changed in order to protect their identities. However, if there is any resemblance to any person, it is purely coincidental.

Contents

Foreword

We all love success stories – stories of courage and larger than life spirits; but how many of us, today, really look at the challenges before us as an opportunity to test the fire of our spirits? How many of us surface from the self-pity that we consciously, out of choice, subject ourselves to? How many of us question the fragmented social fabric and its imbalanced, unpractical assumptions as unfair? How many of us can actually break away from the shackles of the social support mechanism when it actually becomes a tool for the manipulative few? How many of us dare to tackle problems differently? How many of us can look at death in the eye and tell ourselves, 'I will survive'?

Here is a lady who did all that and much, much more. *Silent Echoes* is not just a story. It is a life sketch of courage, conviction and commitment – to values and to life. An ordinary girl with adverse circumstances, but extraordinary grit, teaches us that if nature gives us a lemon it's possible to make a lemonade of it. This book brings out how the lack of maturity of any one partner in a marriage can cause irreparable damage. Marriage is a bond that is built on mutual respect and not on material gifts. There is no substitute for good parental guidance and maturity of judgement.

— *Shiv Khera*

Preface

'Prerna' means inspiration. Words have a lot of power, they never just fade. What starts as a sound ends as a deed. A book is an odd sort of friend. Our friends may change or die, but the words within a book, and the willingness of those very words to make the most beautiful conversation to whoever seeks to read them is never ending.

Prerna's true story stirs the soul of every being who claims to be humane ... it brings forth the cascading images of greed, harassment, torture, pathos, strength and endurance ... it is a heart rending account of her experiences rooted in a crumbling dream of her marital bliss and abiding fight for her identity. I can say without an iota of doubt, that Prerna's journey to find her own essence would surely be an eye opener and inspiration for the fair sex in particular. Prerna's story is the struggle against the erosion of the Hindu ideal of marriage.

I find in myself an amalgamation of many of Prerna's characteristics as I set out to write about her life. I dive into the depths of other people's suffering of all types. I see a reflection of myself and Prernas in every cancer patient I happen to meet, every disabled person I see, and every divorced, single parent who is striving to bring up his or her child. All of these characteristics that are components of me help me to understand and appreciate people from many walks of life.

In England, Prerna suffered in the short space of three to four years, the terrible experience of a hundred years, ever since she came into contact with her in-laws. Her marriage was a plot by them to loot her family. At the failure of such a plot, both her husband and his relatives subjected Prerna to verbal and physical abuse. Comparing other girls' dowries to hers was a common topic of discussion which was followed by more abuse and cursing of her family in her presence.

During these times, Prerna lost her health, happiness, identity and her will to live. She developed cancer and was thrown out like an obsolete object, of no use to anyone. Her lack of knowledge of the existing British laws about dowry, meant that she lost all of her material belongings to her in-laws in addition to the dowry she did take with her. It is only now that I understand that the things that can be bought can just as easily be thrown away, as Prerna has accumulated enough in her life to be happy.

The thought of anyone else going through what Prerna did keeps me awake at night. Dowry is the bane of Asian society and the marital system that this society has constructed. It compelled me to express her affliction and agony in print. It's almost like an auction, in which the son is sold to the highest bidder. Even after that, I wonder if the parents' greed can ever be satisfied.

By writing this book, I convey my understanding of life to all those who take the time to learn from Prerna's harrowing experiences. It is an appeal to all young ladies, who like Prerna are becoming victims of the society that has been designed to be prejudiced against them. It is a request to the boys' parents who subject their children to the dowry system and the pain and grief that is often associated with it. A daughter or daughter-in-law is no less a human being than a son, and I wish that parents could accept and love her just like their sons.

I hope that parents can accept their children regardless of their gender and allow their children to choose their own paths in life. Parents must stop putting their children under spotlights of cruelty in the guise of culture, tradition and customs just to please themselves. Our future educated generations should be free to choose and be independent.

My hopes also extend further: I write for those cancer patients who like Prerna, are on the brink of giving up, of giving in to the illness that demands so much strength from them that it becomes difficult to decide which is more worthwhile, living or dying. We all have something to live for, it is simply a matter of recognising it.

Amita Malhotra

Acknowledgements

Any work carries the imprints of many people around the writer. This work has also been possible because of the reflections of the actions and emotions of those around me. I am grateful to life for giving me an opportunity to meet those who have influenced me and for the events that have taught me. I express deep gratitude to all. I acknowledge my gratitude to the following people:

To my mother and father, who shaped me into the person I am, with kind and loving touches throughout my life.

To my siblings and their families, without whom I could not have faced the hardship that life sprung at me. Their prayers and efforts were my strength to cope with cancer. May God bless them today and always.

To my son Mohit, who forms the first thought in my mind in the morning and the last thought at night, the child who always smiled through life's hardest times and gave me a reason, as well as the strength, to carry on writing. Thank you, for putting in the time to edit this book, with the help of your good friend, James Williamson. May you always shine like the star that you are and tread the path of love, happiness, success and jubilation in life.

To Dr J A Tappin, for giving me a second chance in life, one which gave me the opportunity to see my son grow and realise the true meaning of being alive.

To Dr and Mrs Marcus, whose words alone uplift the soul and enlighten the mind. Thank you for the many hours of your valuable time that you sacrificed to listen and share your insights on all of my problems.

To Mr and Mrs Shiv Khera, thank you for introducing me to sterling publishers and giving me all the help in making my dream come true. Your help will always be acknowledged and appreciated.

To Mr R P Sengupta, whose debt I can never repay, the man who conceptualised this book and encouraged me to publish it.

To Mathieu Lava, who in hard times in his own life, and amidst his own studies, would stay with me in a silent corner of the house, typing away late into the night, to form the foundations of this book.

To Aileen Carrick and Lavinia Hayes, thanks cannot express the feeling I have for you. You have both seen me through the worst and best of times, and if I had to choose anyone who truly knows who I am and what I am capable of as a person, I would have to nominate both of you every time.

To Niedhie Verma, thank you for everything. May God bless you today and always.

To Jaya Vatsyayan, thank you for the words that gave meaning to my thought.

Last but most definitely not least, I thank from the depth of my being, my soul, all those doctors, nurses, social workers, carers and cancer groups that have made Prerna both willing and able to stand at the heights she has reached today.

To all those who have inspired Prerna to take charge of her life, I would love to name you all, but space constrains me from doing so.

1
Back Home

Who is she? This is a question that has often lost me to the deepest of thoughts. How time has flown between what she was and what she is today, sitting here before me. Her life, that seemed to lack inspiration, now reaching new heights. My ears are attentive to every word as her tale unfolds before me. Herein lie the words that Prerna spoke ...

It's morning. I open my eyes to the beams of light seeping through the gap in the curtains, taking a few moments before realising where I am. It's Christmas time and I'm back in India, like every Christmas that has preceded this one, and inevitably like every Christmas I will experience in future. It's different this time; I'm used to the company of my son, my parents, and my friends. I look around me, knowing that I'm all alone, the only sounds gracing my ears being the bustle of the routine of the street outside my window, and the familiar clatter of dishes, as the helper prepares my morning tea.

I walk quietly to the window. It's colder this year than most. I feel it running through my being, stiffness creeping through me, that familiar ache, knowing that to even shed a tear may break past the tolerance for pain that I have. My dressing gown trails along the floor behind me as I wrap it around myself as best I can. I pull open the balcony door, a cold breeze soothing my eyes as I watch silently, in awe, looking at those streets, the same streets that as a child I carelessly ran through all those years ago. My eyes sliding shut, slipping away into the depths of my memory, I see life how it once was.

Bequeathing handsome properties to my father, Rishi Dev Malhotra, affectionately known as Laji, who was then just three years old, my grandfather left for his heavenly abode. My father was, however, fortunate to have my grandmother as the matriarch of the family, a woman whose touch moulded him.

A man of large fortune, my father could easily have afforded a commodious mansion, but he preferred to live in a small three storey house. This was simply due to the proximity of the house to his office, from which he conducted all of his affairs in relation to the business that he had inherited in Ludhiana, a region of Punjab in northern India.

We lived in a bazaar, a busy and noisy place. The home was modest, and after walking but twenty yards into the market, was visible on the left-hand side.

Ludhiana is best known for woollen mills and for being an industrial town with a wealthy population. It has many private schools, colleges and temples, because of which Ludhiana is a busy community, full of educated people.

I was brought up alongside two brothers and two sisters, by parents who insisted that our upbringing be that of upstanding Hindus, in accordance with all of our traditions. From the child that I once was, to as I see my parents today, my understanding, my perceptions and my choice of expressions to describe my family, have undergone some changes.

In my youth, I saw my father as a gentleman, loving and kind for the most part, quiet in his day-to-day life. He was an honest man, as every businessman should be, incredibly humble and soft-spoken, and a true well-wisher to all. A

16

man who would never accept second-best for himself or his family, an example that would be most prominent in my mind would be his dress sense. He was immensely particular in this aspect, wearing only the finest woven and tailor made garments, which at the time were a symbol of the wealthy.

However, there was a side of him that often became irritable and even angry at times. Discipline was essential, when under his roof. It is a fair comment that he would not accept second best for us, but he would never tolerate second best behaviour from us either. Looking back however, I find this very side of him to be the one that shaped my own character the most, and can only smile when thinking of the strength and conviction he possessed. Oddly enough, as far as my mother is concerned, I think the opposite.

My mother Sheila was concerned with two things in life, religion and her family, regardless of what this may mean. Her hours would be spent at prayer, mostly before the household had even awoken. Her other time was divided amongst us, never kept for her own means. Her caring nature aside, the most striking thought in hindsight is that she remained with my father, and in doing so was the epitome of an Indian wife at the time. I say this because my father was an alcoholic, and often one that was hard to cope with.

Growing up as one of five siblings has its perks, as well as its downsides, but I mostly look back at the relationship we had then with the fondest of memories.

My sisters, Dinki and Sawi were the eldest of the five, with only a year separating them. They were eight and seven years older than me respectively, and because of this, in the earlier years of life we had very little common ground with which to relate to one another. I feel now that even when I began to mature in life, I was always seen by them as a child, which was often to my distaste as in general my views and thoughts were not given space in their world.

My brothers however, Manu and Ballu, were the ones that I really grew up with, and by this I mean the ones I fought the most with, which I suppose is the main characteristic in such relationships, and inevitably forms close bonds in time.

Because of the size and closeness in the family, my childhood was never a lonely time. Since there were five of us in the house, and I hasten to add, in the same room when it came to sleeping, there was always someone to argue with, if and when all else failed.

Our Munimji, the equivalent of an accountant, but to be entirely honest, the biggest 'yes' man in my father's life, was always a welcome addition to the family home, along with Dad's two school friends, Thapar Uncle and Murti Uncle, who were like brothers to him.

This closeness extended to their families, whom I remember spending summer holidays with, as we often went away together. When looking back I feel that a true passion in my father's life was that of spontaneous travel.

I clearly remember the Ganges, my father's favourite place to visit at Haridwar, worshipped by Hindus for its holy water. Coincidentally this was the one place where I remember my father never touching alcohol. Possibly for this reason I can call him a devout Hindu even today.

In the evening, I would stand on the white bridge, statues of elephants adorning either side, watching the *aarti*, a prayer ritual that priests carry out morning and evening with hundreds of lighted lamps on leaves, floating on the water. The lamps made the water look like liquid gold, flowing at its fastest. The sound of water was like a newly-wed bride running with heavy ankle bells on her feet. People chanted in the same tune and stood still, watching the *aarti* being performed to the accompaniment of hundreds of clanging bells and chanting of hymns. The atmosphere in Haridwar was completely charged with the prayers, lights and the glimmering Ganges.

I remember wearing soft cotton dresses and Bata flat sandals. We bathed every morning in the Ganges and always found something to laugh about, most commonly when other women's petticoats would float high above their waists as they dipped into the water, comically, yet very religiously chanting *Jai Gangey*. We would tie mangoes in a cloth and hold it in the ice-cold rapids, cooling them to eat while bathing. Our holidays were always a welcome distraction from the busy life we led at home.

I feel another characteristic of my childhood, especially the earlier years, was one of illness. I would often have high fever in the mornings and evenings, commonly due to the changing seasons. To the envy of my siblings, this meant that I spent a lot of time at home, whilst they did not possess quite such a fine excuse to miss school.

A two-minute walk away from home was the doctor's clinic, comprising one room, and every day that I missed school, my mother would make it a point to take me there. One side contained patients, some coughing, others violently blowing their noses. The secretary would occupy one small corner, taking names and arranging the queue. The doctor's table would be at the very back of the room, surrounded by all kinds of implements, practically everything required for 'first aid', or the equivalent of it when I compare it to Britain. When I look back at this now, I find it almost unbelievable. However the situation today has not changed. I remember that for my illnesses, I was given injections twice a day, which would be administered in my thigh. Being as young as I was, it was of course very painful, and I vividly recall the genuine love and affection of both my parents through this period.

I slept with my parents until I was around six or seven. I feel now that I didn't wish to part from them. I enjoyed their affection to such an extent that I couldn't fall asleep unless I was with them. I know now they had their own ways in which they looked after me. My mother often stayed awake at night, running her fingers through my hair until I fell asleep, and my father, who in all honesty would spoil me, had dresses made for me, and gave me plenty of money to enjoy whatever childhood desires I might have had.

I remember at night, Dad would often drink in his bedroom, as Mum put me to sleep. I would fall asleep listening to Dad's music, mostly Hindi film songs by Mohammed Rafi or Lata Mangeshkar (two very famous Indian singers). I would fall asleep to the smell of his alcohol, and the smoke of his cigarettes. However, I would awaken to the smell of incense, and my mother's praying as it was the same room. This, at the time was not unusual to me, but today, it is almost as if these cues, hearing that music, or smelling that incense, takes me back to those childhood days.

During childhood, I had lots of dreams and was always looking forward to fulfil them. My most prominent dream however, was to be married, a dream that I feel stemmed from Dinki's wedding in 1972 to Billa. I was eight years old when she was married, making her a mere sixteen, and the event was the most wonderful I had seen. The marriage was on the recommendation of my paternal aunt, known as *Bhuaji*. Since Indian families view daughters as a liability, or rather, guests in their parents' homes, until they enter their true homes, that of their husbands, the marriage proposal for Dinki was accepted as soon as it was made.

It was a festive occasion for all our family members and friends, and they involved themselves enthusiastically in decorations, religious ceremonies, rituals, and sumptuous feasting. Dinki was very fortunate to have a handsome and caring husband and a mother-in-law who was full of affection for her new daughter-in-law. The addition of a male member in the family, as a son-in-law to my parents, and a fond brother-in-law (*jijaji*) to us brothers and sisters, was very welcome. The birth of a daughter, Vandu, to Dinki in 1974, marked another round of celebration in my family. I thoroughly enjoyed helping Dinki dress Vandu, feed her and take her out in a pushchair.

However, festivities aside, the rest of us were thoroughly enjoying our school lives at this time, while Sawi had entered college at the time of the wedding.

2

My Teenage Years

The year 1977 was a turning point in my life. My mother had to go abroad to her brother, whom I called Mani Uncle, accompanied by my two elder sisters, for Sawi's treatment. Sawi was born with a large black mole on her forehead. She had to undergo skin grafting to remove it. All these years, I had seen her adopt a particular hairstyle, not so much out of a sense of aesthetics, but as an effort to cover the black patch. With their departure, I had to shoulder greater responsibilities in the family, which included looking after my father, grandmother, brother-in-law and two brothers.

The onus of running the household and catering to the needs of all, fell on me. Grandmother was on the wrong side of sixty and the other members being males, the privileged ones, I had to be at their beck and call, attending to their needs. Yet my every attempt was to be a dutiful daughter to my parents.

It was during this period that a physical disturbance, which was a mystery to me, tortured my physique. Since sex education in school as well as in family circles was taboo, I was completely unaware of the disturbances and aches that the arrival of puberty in a girl can bring about. However, my grandmother came to my rescue to illumine me about the developments that take place in a female when she enters womanhood from girlhood.

When my mother and Dinki returned, Sawi stayed back in England with Mani Uncle, for further treatment. I was happy to have Mum back and pleased with the gifts she had brought for me from England. During this time, as I myself was somewhat maturing, Dinki became very friendly with me and I grew close to her. I loved watching her dress up and apply make-up.

These years also saw my transition from junior school, Rama Model School, to Jain Girls High Secondary School. This transition was a topic upon which my father and I had differences. My brothers went to co-educational private schools. My sisters went together to a different school that was for girls only. Seemingly, Dad's favourite pastime was reading the worst possible scenarios of abuse against women that he could find in the daily newspaper, at the top of his voice. I suppose he did this to make me aware that women in this society needed more protection than men. Although this had some logic, it did not satisfy me because I could not understand why I could not go to a good co-educational school. Deep down inside, I enjoyed fighting with Manu and Ballu so much, and I was so much closer to them than I was to my sisters, that I wanted to go to school with them.

Obviously, this was not an argument that I had any chance of winning. Mine was a school only for girls. I settled down in my school, accepting that my father was simply looking after my interests. In school, music rapidly became my favourite subject. I had always been exposed to music around the house, so I suppose this was a natural progression. I had four very close friends in school, and I vividly recall our lunchtime get-togethers, to sing our favourite songs, while nibbling whatever lunch we had packed that morning. Music gave me a release from both scholastic and home life. When I sang, it almost felt as if I could soar freely, like a bird. I had no boundaries whatsoever. I was free.

Santosh Behenji, my music teacher, was of course my favourite. Not only because the subject was my favourite, that goes without saying, but she also impressed me to such an extent, that even today I think very fondly of her. Santosh Behen Ji was blinded in her childhood, and for forty years, had been teaching music at my school. She had taught for so long in fact, that she taught my mother music around 25 years before she taught me. She only wore white sarees with a white shawl. I see her as a vision of purity, and her musical talent was second to none. It seems as though, despite her disability, she seemed comfortable with most musical instruments. I remember her playing the harmonium the most, but she could just as easily pick up a sitar, and play it perfectly.

In 1978, Dinki gave birth to her second daughter, Jasmine, whom we affectionately called Jo. As time rolled by, another landmark event in the family took place in 1980, with the return of my sister, Sawi, from England. Having spent two years there for her treatment, she was a completely changed person. Her groomed beauty, etiquette, and cultured demeanour made her the centre of attention of all eyes. A beautiful blend of the East and the West in her personality made her an enviable person.

Since family ties had been established in the U.K., my parents thought of settling my elder brother Manu in England, as they had heard and seen the opportunities available abroad. The relationship between my father and brother was affected due to my father's drinking habit, so in some sense, I feel my mother wished for Manu to stay with her brothers, rather than at home.

That same year, my parents went to England. They had decided to marry Manu to a non-resident Indian girl named Sanju, who had British citizenship. Having found a suitable match for him through Mani Uncle, the marriage was solemnised finally in May 1980. The marriage of a brother is always a most cherished and waited-for ceremony for the

24

sisters. But none of us sisters could make it to the occasion. I stayed back, this time with both my sisters, my brother-in-law, Billa, and my younger brother Ballu. I wished I had gone to England as well. I fussed a lot as it was my turn to go, because both my elder sisters had been to England, but I didn't have a passport. My sisters were so close to each other that they looked like twins. They would always talk all day to each other and I felt left out, as if they did not need me and did not love me. They took my work around the house for granted. Looking back, I realise they may not have meant it that way. I was the youngest and they would call me if they needed anything, and I would run and get it. I did not dare refuse them because my mother was not there to support me. I do not think I was close to anybody at that time. I could not wait for my mother to come back to tell her about what I perceived as my ill treatment, and thus lighten my heart.

Being satisfied with the compatibility and adjustment of Manu and Sanju, my parents returned to India in July 1980. Their return after the marriage ceremony of Manu should have been an occasion of felicitations but destiny wished it otherwise. Joys and sorrows seem to go hand in hand in this life. My paternal aunt (*Bhuaji's*) eldest son, Saina, passed away with a fatal heart attack just before my parents returned. I feel that Saina was definitely the child most loved by my father, as he was born first amongst us children. It was a tragedy too deep for tears. It was a period of mixed emotions – my brother getting married on one hand and my cousin dying suddenly on the other. I did not know whether to be happy or sad. The state of mind of everyone, including myself, made me completely forget to tell anyone about my experiences when my mother was not there. Looking back, I think I became more independent, and in some sense, a shift occurred from my previously extroverted nature, to a newly developed, introverted nature. I kept things inside, and that made me grow up. It made me a thinker. I worried, loved, and cared for everybody, till Mum and Dad came back. I

25

thought there was nothing more for me to worry about. I thought, 'I will be fine now'. I continued my studies at college and did well.

Dinki then had her third daughter, Simran, in November 1980, with whom I shared a special bond, both of us being the third daughter of our parents. The Western world has no idea how a third daughter is seen in the Indian family and in society. As mentioned earlier, a daughter is purely a burden to her parents, because they know that her arrival means that a dowry must be put aside. I was told that at my birth, my grandmother, my father's mother, quite comically counted the number of daughters that my mother had given birth to, and was shocked at having so many daughters in the family. Ironically, she made the same comment to Dinki, at the birth of Simran.

Some relief was given to my grandmother after Manu had his first son, Tuli, in 1981. Many people saw the bottom of huge bottles of champagne, that being my first drink, or at least so my father thought. In 1982, Mum went to England to help Sanju, Manu's wife, with her second baby boy, Vaz. Upon her return she brought Tuli to India, whom the whole family was thrilled to see, especially my grandmother, of course.

As Mum resumed charge of household affairs, I was able to devote myself to academics and extra-curricular activities, which included painting, paper and silk flower-making, singing, and embroidery. My father adored all my creative work in those days. All this helped in the growth of my personality, and helped develop the love for creative arts that has always been an element of my essential identity.

At the same time, I began to notice a big difference between a man and a woman in Indian culture. During this period itself, I became aware of the deep-rooted gender bias in my society. A female is considered a liability from her birth till her death. The arrival of a male child is celebrated with pomp and show, leading to festivities of all kinds, whereas the arrival of a girl child throws the family into

26

depths of despair. A girl's parents have been looked down upon in Indian society as lesser mortals and inferior human beings. In addition to this, the dowry custom makes the birth of a female a losing proposition. Further, even after marriage, there is no guarantee of her future happiness. On the pretext of incompatibility and maladjustment in the family of her in-laws, she stands exposed to the looming threat of divorce, physical and mental abuse.

Even with the advancement of science and technology, spread of education and awakening amongst the masses, a woman's life has maintained the status quo. There is bias and discrimination against her even at her place of work.

Moreover, Indian parents think that since sons are the real descendants, who will carry on the family name, and will have to be the breadwinners in future, their upbringing and education must be of a higher quality as compared to those of daughters. Consequently, the upbringing of daughters is confined to providing her with expertise in running household affairs, and doing household chores only. My parents were not different from other members of Indian society in this approach and attitude.

Parents feel that doling out a handsome dowry at the time of marriage absolves them of their duties towards their daughters. Indian parents also carry on the bias against their daughters by believing that by accepting dowry at the time of the marriage, a daughter automatically surrenders her claim to the ancestral property. It is unfortunate that in spite of the spread of education, awakening and enlightenment among the members of society, by and large, the bridegroom's parents have remained as greedy as their ancestors. A good education, qualities of head and heart and possession of beauty and culture have little value in the eyes of a girl's in-laws—these do not compensate for the lack of dowry. The rich try to fulfil the demands of dowry, but what about the poor? Realising that the amount of dowry is going to be the sole criterion of good relations between the two families, parents pay little attention to their daughter's education and upbringing. In Sawi's case, however, she had everything to keep her happy: education, personality and dowry.

Sawi was married in May 1983. I did not like the family from day one, most likely because I felt Sawi's suitor was in no way as eloquent, or matching in personality to her. However, Sawi's plastic surgery was considered a stigma and finding a suitable match was difficult because of her skin grafting.

There is a Hindi film, *Satyam Shivam Sundaram*, which carried a lot of meaning for my parents, especially my father. In the film, there is a beautiful young girl, not unlike my sister in her youth. The girl is always singing and happy. However, one day, she has an accident with boiling oil, that scars half of her face. From then on, she always keeps half of her face covered. When the girl grows up, a young man falls in love with her. Captivated by her voice and the beauty that he could see, he immediately asks to marry her. One night after the marriage, he discovers the other side of her face, and horrified, he rejects her, beginning to hate the mere notion of being close to her. He begins to blame her for not disclosing her flaw before their marriage. As it can be seen, this movie was not far from the truth in my sister Sawi's case, and thus my father was always honest about her surgery with any potential suitor.

Since I was young at the time, I could never understand why my father would agree to a marriage with the family in question. At the time I found them to be uneducated, when compared to my sister, and they seemed to be immensely backward in thought, whereas Sawi herself was increasingly modern.

I understand now why finding a match for Sawi was a difficult task for my parents. In a marital system which demands perfection, because of my parents' integrity and honesty, they chose to be upfront about Sawi's surgical procedure. In Indian society, there's a tendency that if an arranged marriage does not work out for whatever reason, the go-between gets blamed. No one wished to aid us in finding a suitor, as Bhuaji did in Dinki's case. I feel that no one wanted to accept the blame if the relationship they recommended didn't work out, or perhaps they didn't wish to test the wrath of my father.

3

The Move to England

After Jain High School, I moved on to S.D.P College, Ludhiana. I finished my Bachelor of Arts in Music in August 1983. Almost instantly, I received word from England that Manu had settled down, opening his second clothing shop, and had a house in Gosforth Square, Newcastle. Manu had sent me an invitation to his sons' *mundan,* a ceremony in which the child's hair is shaven. It is a Hindu custom that all boys are, shall I say, subjected to. Anyway, I was advised by the elders in the family that it would be an opportunity to see the function, and help my brother with anything he needed. I suppose I was glad to go. Deep down I had always wanted to visit England, as my sisters had done before me. Also I was looking forward to meeting my sister-in-law, Sanju, and Vaz, neither of whom I had met before. The only fact that saddened me was leaving behind my friends and family, most of all my nieces, whom I adored, a feeling which I genuinely felt was reciprocated.

In September 1983, before I left to be with Manu, I celebrated my birthday, taking my best friends to the cinema and hosting a party afterwards. I was nineteen years old and this was the best birthday I had ever had. I knew deep down that it may be the last birthday amongst my friends in college. Sadly, amidst my festivities, I was rushed here and there to different offices to get my passport. It felt terrible to leave all my friends, and to be absent at the B.A. degree presentation ceremony and the other functions at college. I missed the farewell parties as well. I could not tell any of my friends that I was going to England. There is a popular belief that people who go abroad become so accustomed to the superior quality of life there, that they have no wish to return. However, I hoped to be back soon enough for my friends not to notice my absence.

I collected all of my fondest memories, tied them around my heart and got on to the plane with Karamjeet Nayyar Uncle, Mum's brother-in-law. I landed in Heathrow Airport and Manu came from Newcastle to London to receive me. I was the first member of the family from India to step into his brand new beautiful navy blue Audi. Nothing felt different about England that I had not already heard about, apart from the big lorries which carried ten cars. I did not look at England as a place I wanted to see or somewhere I wanted to live or spend my life. It was simply an opportunity for me to be with Manu.

Looking around and driving from Heathrow Airport to Newcastle, I couldn't help immediately noticing a vast difference between New Delhi and London airports in terms of size, cleanliness, lighting and service. Afterwards we drove to Newcastle, and I, like a child was amazed to see the motorway, the lane system and traffic rules and regulations. How clean everything was! I could not see even a speck of dust anywhere, whereas in India, there is no motorway, no road sense and no regulations. The next thing I noticed was the structure and design of the buildings and the identical houses and rooftops. I realised how far behind India was, how poorly designed our houses were, and how different each house looked from the others in Indian streets.

On the first of October, 1983, I arrived at Manu's home in Newcastle. I met my two lovely nephews, Tuli and Vaz, and Dinki's second daughter Jo, now aged four. She had been here since last year and was very pleased to see me. How adorable, cute and lovely they were to me. I almost forgot my homesickness for a while. Jo had grown and changed so much

31

that I could not recognise her. She looked different. Sanju, as I had seen in photographs, was good-looking. She had beautiful, dark, long hair. She did her best to make me comfortable. Manu welcomed me. Time went on getting to know and fitting into my surroundings and making the most of life. I helped Sanju and Manu with everything they wanted me to do around the house and the shops. Although Sanju and I were both Hindus, her British upbringing meant there were a lot of differences in our understanding of life. I loved the way she spoke Punjabi and tried to accommodate me.

In January 1984, Jo flew back to India to her parents. My father came to England to bless my two nephews on their mundan ceremony. I was old enough to understand that my father's drinking was affecting the whole family now. I knew him as the lovely and kind man he always was with me, but I began to see the other side of him, the person he became when he drank. All the functions that Dad had hosted so far were functions for his daughters, where it would not be appropriate for him to drink. This function was for his grandsons, where there were no such restrictions. Sanju and I wore similar *lehangas* that Dad had got for us in different shades.

I was looking forward to returning to India with my father, but he left without me. Later I learned it was because the idea of my getting married in England would suit the family better; firstly, because Manu would have me here as a family member, and secondly because it would satisfy my parents to have both of us in England.

I wrote a few letters to my mother, pleading with her to call me back to India as I had no intention of getting married as yet. I did not like staying in England, and that is most definitely putting it politely. I did not like the Indian people living in England. The weather was too cold and the idea of being a working woman here was vastly different from the Indian housewife that I had always wanted to be. But despite my feelings, I had to obey my family's wishes. I felt trapped, missing my home and friends and longing to continue my education with them. With my immature observation, I saw the world that day, that way. By now, I had been in England for nearly seventeen months. I carried on with life, taking note of everything around me. I was noticing the difference between the country where I was born and the country where I was to live from now on. I then thought that I had the maturity to understand the vast differences between the two. Subconsciously, I started to compare. In England, people are extremely independent, polite and helpful. Whereas in India, interference in other people's affairs is a common practice.

Gossiping in India is common and considered the best way to pass time. In my own experience I felt English people are very open-minded and straightforward about their good and bad feelings. In India, people believe in facades and formalities all the time. A person is given special treatment on account of his wealth and property in India. If you happen to be poor in India, you automatically have no rights and are not even considered a human being. In England, the legal system is entirely different. There is no bribery in any office you enter.

There is hardly any similarity between the Indian and English way of life. The climate, surroundings, culture, administration, educational pattern, morals and ethical values are completely contrary to each other, and this is an observation of 1983. I won't even go into the differences today. "East is East and West is West and never the twain shall meet," had been rightly observed by Rudyard Kipling.

The redeeming feature of Indian society is the adherence to the institution of the family. Amongst Indians even at present, there is a conscientious observance of high moral standards. Indians show a profound respect for their elders, esteem for womenfolk and attachment to their children. In their moments of grief, they console one another and in festivities they share their happiness and joy. No one feels lonely or in want of company. In England, however, there is a sharp degeneration of the institution of the family.

I was brought up with a certain image of womanhood. Seeing women drinking and smoking and showing their bare skin was an image that could not even be conceived in the society I came from, and I was shocked to see it as commonplace.

Even though I appreciated certain facts like cleanliness, independence, security of British law and technical innovations, it still wasn't my lifestyle. My heart felt lonely because I missed the amicability of India, the family bonds that transcend generations, the security of going to someone your age and talking your heart out. England walked too fast to keep pace with my emotions. This is how I compared the two countries and saw good, bad, right, wrong through my immature mind.

4
My Marriage

As the presence of an unmarried daughter hangs heavy on the minds of parents in India, they always keep a lookout for an opportunity to bind her in wedlock. My parents were no exception to this. A traditional Indian girl would be a desirable prospect for British-Indian parents, as they would want to marry their sons with someone who would stick to the Indian standards that are set, and not veer off into British culture. It also enabled their family name to be carried on with dignity, especially if the girl was of a good family background. It had long been my desire to marry in India, and there alone. British life was fine indeed, but not at all compatible with me. My parents however thought it would be more beneficial for me to marry in England, and they conveyed these wishes to Manu, telling him to keep an eye out for a suitable match.

My visa was due to expire in March 1985, and if I wanted to remain in the country, I would have to get married before this date, to someone with British citizenship. So, in January, Manu, alongwith Aunt Nirmal, who is my mother's sister, and Sehgal Uncle, her husband, took me to Liverpool to meet a family that they had found to be suitable.

We were greeted in Liverpool by one of Manu's friends, Virender, an elderly man who had introduced my family to the family in which I was to be married. We stayed with

Virender for the duration of our trip. His house was truly impressive. The outside was very grand, and I remember the large and expensive cars that graced the driveway.

We were welcomed into the lounge, and Virender introduced us to two handsome young men and their parents, who were a seemingly nice middle-aged couple. While being introduced to them, I was immensely shy in front of these strangers, knowing that if all went well as Manu wished, these were to be my in-laws, my new family. My eyes were constantly downcast, pondering which of the two brothers Manu had in mind for me. When they did flicker upwards to steal a glance, I noticed a constant smile on one of their faces, a smile that I liked from the outset.

Before any real conversation could be initiated, Aunt Nirmal whisked me away to show me the house, as well as offer any reassuring words she could. She enthusiastically showed off a large bar, a snooker room and a pool table, as well as a tennis court. I vividly remember the bedrooms, and how finely they were decorated.

When entering the kitchen, I found one of the young men and his mother, my mother-in-law-to-be, sitting at the table. The young man was not the one who had smiled at me. I was later to learn that he was the younger of the two, Bajiv I was here to meet the elder, Sajan.

Sajan's mother, Kusha, began with quite a standard topic, to my relief, the weather. She soon veered onto my education however, wanting to know the extent to which I could speak English. I later realised the surreptitious intention in her questioning. Deep down I knew, that the only desire these people had was for a daughter-in-law who was educated enough to speak English. I know now that what really motivated them to consider this proposal, was my father's wealth. After this brief introduction, Sajan slipped away with his mother, telling her that he was happy enough to proceed with this marriage. I, however, was the converse. I obviously didn't want to get married in England, that much was apparent. The only consolation to me would be to find a partner who was highly educated, someone whom I could converse with on an intellectual level. Sajan had all that a girl seeking material possessions could desire, but in my eyes, his O-level education was at a much lower standard than what I had hoped for. I, however, much to my regret today, remained silent. I felt that my parents' wishes, and Manu's effort, as well as the atmosphere around me, was too powerful for me to speak up against. I didn't want to disappoint anyone by rejecting this marriage proposal. When Manu asked me for my opinion, all I could say was, 'as you wish'. He held my hand, trying to reassure me that Sajan was a hardworking man, with a beautiful home, and a grocery business that he ran with his parents. I would have all I needed to be comfortable and happy. I chose to overlook Sajan's lack of education and, looking at the overall picture, I accepted the proposal. I was enamoured by the glitter and out of immaturity, decided to go against my conscience. I fell for the form, overlooking the substance.

We left Liverpool that very evening, with hopes high that the festivities surrounding a marriage would begin soon. Manu rang Dad in India, informing him that I was to be engaged soon, and that everything had been arranged. My father, being of very old-fashioned and traditional views, condemned the marriage immediately, when he heard they were in the grocery business. He believed that this family was lower in status to his own. Dad was apprehensive because he felt that there would be a marked difference in their way of thinking and their lifestyle as compared to our own as landowners. In a typical traditional Indian marriage, people only marry their children into a family of the same status. In these modern days however, as Manu explained to my father, this system was obsolete. Trusting Manu's words and judgement, my father finally agreed to this marriage. I know in my heart, that although I wished for my father to find a match for me, he would not be capable of finding one that would be suitable, because of his well-known alcohol and health problems. The responsibility of my marriage fell on Manu's shoulders, and I know to this day, that he fulfilled that responsibility with all his love and affection for me.

When one has faith in destiny, one realises that individual events are all part of a large scheme, commonly known as life. No individual's approval, disapproval, agreement or disagreement can be considered to have a bearing on the circumstances of life. I am a firm believer in destiny, in the sense that what fate has planned for us, is beyond us. What happened was to happen.

The engagement ceremony was held in Newcastle amongst family and friends. Everyone approved of our match and congratulated us. My dreams of being married started taking form. My registered wedding took place on 26th Jan, 1985. It was a beautiful day. I wore a very heavy Indian saree and very expensive jewellery. Manu hired a Rolls Royce for the whole day. I was very nervous, shaky and sad deep down because my parents, relatives and friends from India were not with me. I was grateful for what Manu did for me. He tried to find me a good match and although it was my father's duty to finance the wedding, Manu bore the expenses. It worried me but he explained that it did not matter who paid, as it came from the same family. Still, it would have pleased me if my father had taken this responsibility.

After that, things started to look different. I was looking forward to becoming a wife and having a loving husband. I wrote to my parents asking them to attend my Hindu wedding ceremony in August 1985, so that my father could give me away and I would try to forget our previous little disagreements over settling down in England. But due to ill health, my father could not travel, so once again, his responsibilities fell on Manu's shoulders.

Sanju and I made lists of shopping and guests and ran in and out of town to get all I desired. Manu had the decor of his house changed and also got the whole house decorated. My nephews Tuli and Vaz loved me much more, knowing I would be going away soon to live in Liverpool.

I found that time was flying by at great speed between January and August of that year. Shopping for my wedding trousseau had begun, and Manu went to India with a list of my favourite colours, returning with sarees, suits and matching jewellery, bringing back exactly what I wanted. Being the last daughter of the family, I was given the best dowry. In Indian culture, dowry means the daughter's share of the father's wealth. Although Dad couldn't travel at all, Mum and Billa, Dinki's husband, flew to England to attend my wedding. This was a point of relief, as the support of these family members was a help in this emotional time. Billa performed the *milni* ceremony (*milni* is a custom where family members of the bride and groom welcome each other with garlands) on my dad's behalf. Aunt Nirmal and Sehgal Uncle gave me away as their daughter.

On the wedding day, 26 August 1985, everyone was so busy preparing, that in spite of their good intentions, I still felt alone. I did not know a thing about make-up or wearing a saree. I missed India and the way my friends would have gathered around, and helped me get dressed. No one here was available to assist me to get ready on my big day. As far as dressing up was concerned, my wedding day remains the worst day in my life. I missed my sisters the most, especially Dinki and her daughters. Manu had spent all his money booking a five-star hotel to provide the best of everything. He hired a Rolls-Royce yet again for the whole day.

All day long, I was surrounded by people, making me very emotionally tense, as I wanted to spend these moments with my close family members. Most of the crowd that attended the wedding meant nothing to me, as I didn't know most of them personally. People came to enjoy the atmosphere created for them with good food, drinks and music at the hotel in Newcastle.

While the festivities were still going on, some realities started unfolding. I painfully discovered a mysterious queerness in my husband and realised that he had never visited India. He neither showed any etiquette during the feasting nor any seriousness during the rituals. Being a pretty Indian girl, belonging to a well-to-do, respectable family, I had pinned high hopes on my husband and in-laws. But Sajan turned out to be hopelessly uncouth and inconsiderate. While I was fasting all day, Sajan was feasting. My family was extending all hospitality to him, which is traditional. Generally the groom's side extends similar hospitality to the bride, which was totally missing.

Sajan did not understand either the meaning of the wedding rituals or a word of what the priest was saying about the responsibilities of a husband and wife. He kept laughing and ridiculing the priest who was performing the rituals. I was marrying someone neither English nor Indian. I did not know what to expect next. When some food was brought to us, I expected Sajan to offer it to me, but instead he quickly started eating without taking any note of my presence. Although I was starving, I could not eat. Sajan completely ignored me all through the day. I looked at Sanju and she gave me a hug and said that I should eat something, but somehow I had no appetite. I was only hoping to be like Dinki and Sanju and be loved by my husband and in-laws. This was my first experience of my husband's lack of seriousness about the relationship.

The DJ then called the newly-wed couple to take the centre stage to dance amongst the crowd. I had never been taught to dance and my shyness did not help. Trying to dance in that heavy outfit surrounded by hundreds of people and without Sajan giving me a hand, made me look a complete fool at my wedding. These steps marked the end of my journey of being a daughter in Newcastle. Feasting and dancing was to be followed by the *doli*, a ceremony of bidding the final adieu to a daughter by her parents and other relatives, blessing her that she may become an integral part of her in-laws' family. During this ceremony they surrender their claim to their daughter and wish her a happy life in her in-laws' home. For every Indian girl, her father's presence at this all-important ritual is much pined for. But the absence of my father on this occasion made me cry inconsolably. This was the end of the first chapter of my life, the one spent at my parents' home. I looked at Manu with pride for doing all that he did for me. I blessed him with all my heart for doing the duty of my father. Soon, it was time to leave with my in-laws and Sajan. I cried a lot all the way to Liverpool without any consolation from anyone. Sajan did not hold my hand or try to comfort me. I felt he was taking an object with him. I was missing home already.

5
Liverpool, My Marital Home

When we arrived at my marital home in Liverpool, I was told to change into an outfit that my in-laws had bought, symbolising that from this day forth, they were taking the responsibility of clothing me, taking me to my new home as their daughter, a loved member of their family. I then had to hand over my money and valuables to Sajan in case I lost them. Nobody knew or cared how tired I was. I had been looking forward to receiving the kind of love and care my parents had given to Sanju. My parents loved Sanju more than their own daughters and respected her in every way.

D. H. Lawrence in his novel, *Sons and Lovers*, has called marriage the second birth. The second birth or the second chapter of my life started with a rude shock, immediately after my arrival at my in-laws' house in Liverpool. I was stripped of every item of my jewellery. My mother-in-law took possession of all the valuables and items of jewellery which I had brought with such fondness from my parents' home. For my bridal night, my in-laws had booked a suite in a hotel in Manchester. Before our departure for the hotel, my father-in-law, Kadam, approached me and said something which in my view was immodest and brazen on the part of a father-in-law. "Forget your sadness, go to the hotel and play the role of a woman with my son in bed."

Being a deeply money-minded person, he implied by his words that the money spent on the room's tariff should be fully availed of to appease the carnal cravings of his son. Being extremely shy, I felt as if the ground had disappeared from under my feet. I was alone with a male for the first time in my life. The words of Kadam resounded. With no sign of love from Sajan since I had been with him, I did not know what to expect, feeling like a virgin about to be raped. His silence and fast driving was frightening me even more.

The next morning, we drove back to Liverpool. On the way back, Sajan mentioned being put off at not getting as much cash as he had expected from my mother. In the daylight, I found myself in a new town. New people, new surroundings, Sajan, his brother Bajiv, Kusha and Kadam, and this house I went into. I realised within two days of my marriage that I was living with the greediest of people. Kusha told me I was not a suitable match for her son, that I was dark and short and that she could have easily found a better wife for him. I now realised that Sajan did not touch me on our first night as I was not loaded with the wealth that he had expected in addition to my dowry. My heart, body and soul were not good enough for him.

Bitten by the dowry bug, dowry-seekers can be found all over the world. Even the change of environment and bounties of wealth bestowed on them by Lakshmi, the Hindu goddess of wealth, fail to bring contentment. Their greed for dowry remains forever insatiable and the thirst for it unquenchable. This world abounds with such dowry-hungry devils. My in-laws had been in England for thirty-five years, but the environment did not change their petty thinking. I was brought up in the modern age, whereas they wanted me to be a daughter-in-law of the 1950s, because that was when they had arrived in England. Both my parents-in-law came from poor backgrounds and had lived in an Indian village. They moved to England to survive. That is why they were so obsessed with money, and did not respect human dignity. Even their son's marriage was a way for them to get money from my parents. I now had to live up to their expectations and behave as 'an illiterate person', rejected on all counts, my looks, my education, purely there to listen to their abuse.

From the third day, I was shown my responsibilities at the grocery shop that Kadam owned. I worked ten hours a day, from 7 to 5, lifting heavy groceries, and then worked as a maid, though labelled as a housewife, without a break till 10 p.m. for five days a week for them. On weekends I worked for Sajan twelve hours a day in his warehouse, lifting heavy cartons and filling his huge van with loads of groceries. In the evenings, I had to carry on with the housework. I never shared even one meal with Sajan. Instead, I cooked and served everyone's meal first and then cleaned up the kitchen before I was allowed to sit down and eat the leftovers. I felt like a slave, a doormat, a dog who had no choice but to wag its tail around the family members to please them. I looked for love by pleasing them and taking on more and more work.

6

Reception and Honeymoon

Flaunting of riches, hypocrisy and ostentation are the hallmarks of the people who are suffering from an inferiority complex. Just to get the stamp of social status, and keep up appearances in society, people observe pompous ceremonies and organise lavish functions. Many a time, in their heart of hearts, they feel sorry about doing that. My in-laws also organised a wedding reception just to keep up with the trend. And later on sent the newly-wedded couple on a honeymoon. My wedding reception was organised with a mean intent – to collect more in the form of gifts and cash from the invited guests. On top of that, they expected that my parents should foot the bill of the reception. So the reception was organised with commercial motives to earn much more than was spent. Evidently, it did not entail any affection for anyone. Another atrocity conducted by my mother-in-law, was to tell my family to give the gifts before hand at home, rather than at the reception hall. Mum, of course, felt this was sensible, as all of her gifts were solid gold, necklaces for myself, and a chain for Sajan. Later, the reception video was used to show that my parents gave me nothing, and thus, I was entitled to nothing.

All presents received from Newcastle and Liverpool, even those from my reception, were kept by Kusha. This allowed her to control me by making me dependent on her financially permanently. My husband was just as greedy as his parents, if not more, and did not hesitate to show his disgruntlement without delay. The day after the wedding reception, Sajan was supposed to take me to see my family in Newcastle, but instead he made an excuse and let Manu take me alone. The routine carried on and he never accompanied me to Newcastle. I was forbidden to telephone Manu, as I was told that it was very costly. Kusha said if Manu wanted to hear from me, he should ring. Each time he rang, my in-laws were very rude to him, accusing him of not giving enough cash at my wedding.

In September 1985, Sajan took me to Austria for our honeymoon. To my immature mind, honeymoon meant an opportunity for the groom to display generosity and love for the wife. But none of that happened. This is usually an opportunity for a couple to come closer and build stronger bonds for life. Every wife expects indulgence and the freedom to shop. But I was denied even ten pence to make a phone call to my mother, informing her about our safe arrival and the happy honeymoon. This led to an altercation between both of us. I charged him with being mean as I had parted with all the cash and gifts given to me by family as *shagun*, at the time of my departure. I had hoped that my husband would meet my cash needs, whenever the need arose. But both my faith and confidence received a severe jolt and the honeymoon turned out to be a very bitter experience. Today I understand that a honeymoon is meant for the newly-weds to share their bodies and souls. Although we shared bodies, we could not share our souls. On my second day in Austria, my mother was leaving England for India, so I asked Sajan once again for ten pence to make a call to wish her a safe journey home. He behaved as if I had asked him for the moon. He said that the phone was for emergencies and he would only give me ten pence if someone had died. I again reminded him of the hundreds of pounds that I had given him on my first night in their home. He denied and said I had not done any such thing. This argument made me unsure whether I should trust him. I felt like a bird trapped in a cage that nobody needed any more. Away from home, I was trying to find some love between us, that would be necessary for our marriage to survive in his parents' home. Instead, I found that he was with me purely to 'get his money's worth' He was constantly putting a price tag on emotions.

When we got back from Austria, my mother had already left and the rest of my family in Newcastle thought I would be fine and soon find my balance in life. My parents-in-law started shouting at me when they found out that I had asked Sajan for ten pence and that I had called him mean, when he refused to give it. They told me that in future he would never accompany me anywhere out of town.

The workload got heavier and everyone tried to use me as much as they could. I never got any wages, so I had no financial independence whatsoever. The rules in the house were very strict for me. I could not go to my bedroom without permission. If I needed to buy anything for myself, I was told to ask Kadam, who would see for himself whether the need was justified. It put me through a great deal of embarrassment all the time, having to ask my father-in-law for everything, including items for basic personal hygiene.

A new phase of life had started since our return from our honeymoon. Sajan showed complete lack of decency and trust by publicly talking of moments of privacy that are usually kept between a couple. Every behaviour and conversation reflected cheapness, indecency, pettiness, lack of human dignity and poor upbringing. My decency prevents me from saying any more but the reality goes way beyond these words. 'Mean' is a very mild word to describe his behaviour in sharing the details of our honeymoon with his family members. My use of the word 'mean' gave them a finer excuse than their previous ones that I was not beautiful enough and didn't bring enough dowry. They started to form a list of such faults, using them to abuse me more. Now I began to be subjected to physical torture in addition to mental torture. They started looking upon me as their enemy rather than a daughter-in-law whose petty failings or utterings ought to be overlooked. No more did they consider me a part and parcel of their family. For them I was a helpless, deserted slave, obsolete now that I could not give them a larger dowry.

The Indian society in Liverpool that my in-laws socialised with, consisted of about twenty families, mainly very backward old couples, gossiping and comparing dowries and bad-mouthing their daughters-in-law. I was invited with my in-laws to most of their houses for dinner. As a newly-wed member of the society, this was the usual way of getting to know a newcomer in their town. No matter how warm the hosts were to me, the conversation always ended with my in-laws complaining that I did not bring enough cash. People who invited us mostly appreciated my talents, as I was a good singer.

In September 1985, it was my twenty-first birthday, the first since I had been married. My in-laws told everyone that there would be a party, in the hope of more presents from my side of the family, but a day before, an old friend of Kadam died. So the party was postponed. It saved them money and saved me from having to wear another mask in front of society. My in-laws had expected a lot more than I received from my family on my birthday. They picked on me all day for petty things to the extent that even the size of the birthday card from my parents became an issue. My family did send me expensive gifts but nothing was good enough to satisfy their greed. They all made me feel very small and wanted me to accept that my parents were not giving me enough. It was the worst birthday I had ever experienced.

7

Back to India

In December 1985, I was sent to India by my in-laws to shop for Bajiv's wedding. I was also instructed to ask my father to pay for the wedding reception we had in Liverpool. However, the story they spun for the people in Liverpool was different. My in-laws told everyone that I was homesick so they had sent me back to India to allow me to see my family.

My entire family was very excited to have me home for three weeks. My sisters were keen to know about my experiences of married life. Since I remained quiet and smiled, they presumed I was very happy. My grandmother thought the same, but when I tried to tell her that there was not much happiness in my life, she laughed and called me a liar. I laughed with her. My friends were happily married and I hated the thought of being left out. I never showed my unhappiness to anyone, knowing that I would soon leave and they would all be upset if they came to know that I was very lonely and maltreated.

I could see that my mother was very ill. She could not even get up, let alone keep me company or feed me the way she would have wanted, knowing it was my first visit back home to India. Although I was home for the first time after my wedding, and I would have loved to sit with my family, the responsibility of getting clothes and jewels designed for

Bajiv's wedding made me rush during the day and spend sleepless nights. I gave my father Kadam's message demanding money for the wedding reception in Liverpool. But he apologised and said that the family could not accede to such unreasonable demands. My father looked very depressed due to these demands for more dowry and my mother's poor health added to his woes. Dinki and her family were most supportive in every sense and took good care of me.

I also learnt horrific facts of Sawi's life, the first victim of the dowry system in our family. A paragon of beauty as she was, she had gone to her in-laws' house with hopes of a happy, normal life. Having been groomed in England for two years, with a personality that was a superlative blend of eastern and western cultures, she did not know what was in store for her after her marriage. Her in-laws and the uncouth groom had neither any fascination for her beauty nor any appreciation of her well-groomed nature. For them, their greed for dowry could not be compensated by any other virtues of the bride.

This is how the tale of her woes started at her in-laws' house from the day she landed there. Neither did her marriage bring any joy in her own life nor did it bring any relief to our parents. Her in-laws' insatiable demands for items of all descriptions and value, to satisfy their greed for wealth, kept mounting. Every time she visited our parents, it was expected by her in-laws, that she would bring back lots of gifts, bundles of cash as *shagun* (gift), items of jewellery, and the customary food traditionally given to daughters upon visiting their *maika* (parents' home). They had conveniently forgotten the sums of money that Dad had spent on her wedding, and that all their relatives had been suitably honoured with gifts. She was incessantly harassed, starved, rebuked, scolded and cold-shouldered by her in-laws. During her first pregnancy, she didn't get enough nutritious food, let alone proper care. Instead, she was repeatedly sent to her parents' house for prescriptions, medical check-ups and for other medical tests that her pregnancy required. At this juncture, the birth of a male child might have brought some feelings of love in the hearts of her in-laws. She had so many problems during her pregnancy, that the only way for her daughter Anu to be born, was by Caesarean section. The birth of a female child added to her miseries.

Soon after, events in her life took yet another bad turn, when her husband left for Canada to help his brother. With his departure, atrocities were committed on her with greater impunity to the satisfaction of her greedy in-laws. To make matters worse, she was impregnated yet again. Dad's anxiety and Mum's pain for Sawi was breaking them slowly. Sawi felt herself to be a burden on her parents and family because of her own self-respect. In the absence of her husband, Sawi tried to bear all the sufferings in the hope that after her husband returned from Canada, her fortunes would take a turn for the better. In November 1985, once again by Caesarean section, Sawi gave birth to Vanu, her second daughter, in Dad's house. Providence had dealt another blow to her.

I began to see the root of my parents' illness. They could not bear the stress Sawi was being subjected to, and unfortunately, they saw no way out of this situation, and no way of helping their daughter. They kept her in their own home during her pregnancy, paying for all of her medical needs, as well as trying as best they could to please her in-laws. I saw a parallel in Sawi's life, and my own life. When I saw the pain that my parents went through on account of Sawi, I could not bring myself to tell them of the situation that I was in myself, on account of my parents' failing health.

I flew back to England on Christmas Eve, and I had a good cry on the plane. Sajan came to London to pick me up and take me back to Liverpool, back to my cage.

8
Caged

Upon arriving back home in Liverpool, the first question directed at me, was whether or not I had conveyed Kadam's instruction to my father, requesting payment for my wedding reception. I handed him a Fixed Deposit Receipt (FDR) of substantial value. My mother-in-law also took from me the jewellery I was given and the five sarees my father had bought for me. On top of this, my father had also sent clothing for every member of my in-laws' family. This, of course, was not enough. Kadam said that this was substantial only as a gift for my first trip home, not nearly enough for the wedding reception. I was called a beggar's daughter, and told to tell my brother that he owed Kadam money. That very night, Sajan didn't allow me to rest, even for a short while after the long journey. I was put back into my duties, both as a daughter-in-law, as a wife and as a maid servant, all rolled in one.

The next morning was Christmas, and Manu came to Liverpool to surprise me. He brought expensive presents for everyone. I was in so much pain, mentally and physically, that I couldn't even express my feelings of gratitude to him. My in-laws were very cold in their manner towards him, and never offered him even a sip of water in spite of his four hour drive. They came up with the archaic excuse that it is a sin for a brother to eat or drink in his sister's marital home. Upon hearing this, he gave out all of the gifts that he had brought, and left. My choked heart left with him. I sat on the toilet and sobbed. Then I washed my face as if nothing had happened. I kept looking at the gifts Manu had left for everyone and felt heavy knowing that it was too much for me to take, as no one in my in-laws' family deserved any of it.

After a few days I received a letter from India stating that my mother needed a hysterectomy. The letter was also an update of Sawi's situation. Her husband was still in Canada, trying to get a green card there so his family could move across. Her in-laws had refused to keep her, and they were demanding more money from Dad. I worried about my father's situation, whose health was having a downward slide. My father now had five grand daughters, three from Dinki, and two from Sawi. I began to fear for Sawi's health, and was increasingly distressed after learning about the way in which she was being treated.

Life carried on as usual. Bajiv was engaged to Vita, an Indian girl brought up in Malaysia. Vita's family had known my in-laws for the last twenty years. One night, Kadam, when he was drunk, explained to me the reason for choosing me and Vita for his sons. Firstly, I came from a rich family in India and secondly Vita's elder sister was married to one of the wealthiest Indian families in Manchester. Kadam being a man of false values, wanted people to think that he must be very wealthy to have daughters-in-law such as ourselves married to his sons. That way, both his sons would meet the elite of society and be surrounded by wealthy people. His sons would gain a higher status in society.

I clearly understood his actions and motives. It was all a facade, reinforcing my view of how superficial and money-minded this family was. I knew that money does not make people rich but only makes them wealthier. I laughed in my mind at his attitude. Anyway, no matter how I felt inside about my life, I prepared myself to welcome Vita into our home. Vita had no respect for conservative Indian culture.

She visited my in-laws regularly and had a good time with her future husband. So I was aware that she would be closer to my in-laws due to their previous friendship.

I knew for sure that they would treat her differently, as she had a wealthy sister and brother-in-law, her only relatives in England, living twenty miles away from our house. Her brother-in-law would never let them treat her badly, whereas Manu, my only relative in England, could not compete financially with these people and he lived far away. They owned factories while my brother had only a small clothing business. In February 1986, Bajiv and Vita got married.

When Vita arrived, she tried to be friendly. I desperately needed her friendship. Then she started torturing me mentally by hiding my things and was determined to show that she was the better daughter-in-law. Soon I was to realise that it was all play-acting because Vita and Kusha connived to plan and make me work even harder. I obeyed, thinking that one day they would realise my worth and love me. I was constantly told off, slapped and sworn at by my in-laws for not bringing enough when compared to Vita.

I had hoped that Bajiv's marriage to Vita might usher in an era of some relief. But contrary to expectation, the arrival of another daughter-in-law in the family made my life more miserable. The two women opposed me in that house and started malicious machinations jointly to drive me from one misery to another. I can never forget some scenes that happened every night. After I had done all the household chores and cleaned the kitchen before going to bed, as soon as I would touch the door handle of my bedroom, Kusha and Vita would be lying in Kusha's bedroom laughing, joking aloud and singing Punjabi songs to torture me - "*Na kar soniya teri ik parjai weh, na kar soneya eh tah masan basaie weh,*" meaning that I was unfit for this household, yet they had accepted and kept me with a lot of difficulty. Then Kusha would call me, "*Ni dafa honiey. Kum khatam ho giya tan thalle ja hun, dud nu jag lega ke aa.*" It was an order for me, implying that this was my temporary abode and I must go down again, switch on the cooker, boil milk, stand there till it cools, set it to make curd, then wash the pan and clean around again. The ridicule and laughter was loud between Vita and Kusha. If I didn't do what Kusha asked me to do, I knew she would call all the men and they would all scold and beat me for not obeying their orders.

9
Pregnancy and Assault

In March 1986, I found out that I was expecting a baby. It was an expected development as Sajan wanted to be a father before Bajiv. It was not a matter of love or choice, it was something that happened to me. I was very scared but was told not to inform my family till I was seven months pregnant. I was devastated at not being allowed to tell anyone, and carried on my duties as usual.

Wednesdays became my 'day off' during my pregnancy. Sajan, Bajiv, Vita and Kadam would all go to work, leaving me alone with my mother-in-law. I would wake up at the same time however, at around five in the morning, when the rest of the household awoke. I would serve their breakfast, and see them off to work. After they would leave, Kusha would dictate a list of chores that would have to be done around the house. Every Wednesday, she would take a large tub of wax, smearing it thickly over both the twelve seater dining tables, and the six seater kitchen table. She would hand me a cloth, and tell me to scrub it, until all of the wax had been rubbed into the wood, making sure to watch, and point out every minor fault. I would be made to scrub the kitchen floors, even in the last days of my pregnancy. I'd climb on kitchen units to clean all of the tiles until they were shimmering. Once I was even made to mow the lawn outside, and trim all of the plants and hedges. There was every risk of losing the child growing within me but it didn't bother her. She was a sadist and it pleased her when she inflicted pain upon me. She then told me not to tell anyone that I had done the garden, as they may disapprove. When Sajan, Bajiv and Kadam came home, she was lying in bed, saying that she had a headache from doing the garden, and that I had been lying around all day. The stove became a metaphor for my existence. I was turned on at five in the morning, and turned off late at night. Kusha would make sure that at every moment, something was cooking, so not a second's gas was wasted.

One day, I had a terrible backache and Kadam, as usual, moaned in the shop about having me as his daughter-in-law. He told me to fill the shelves over and over again until my backache got unbearable. He then ordered me to fill the shelves with packets of crisps. It meant filling at least twenty different types of crisps. I had to lift and carry each type of box down from a high shelf before making rows from the bottom of the new shelves to the top, stretching and bending for each packet. I was in agony which gave him vicarious pleasure. He asked me to hurry up. I could not say anything and my last resort was to pray to God to note what I was going through.

Other people only saw the smiling mask I wore to please my in-laws and maintain their reputation of being good to me. Each time we had a visitor or we visited someone, my in-laws only had one message: that I did not bring enough. My brother was aware of it and tried telling the people involved in arranging my wedding, including Aunt Nirmal, that my in-laws did not think that he gave enough to me. Manu brought Sehgal Uncle and Aunt Nirmal to speak to my in-laws about the problem. They were made to feel unwelcome and insulted and were told that I had an inferiority complex because Vita had brought more than I did. Manu took me to Newcastle with him for a few days, knowing about my pregnancy. Manu was always by my side to help but even he could not meet the ever-increasing demands of my in-laws. Encouraged by the situation and to keep my in-laws in good humour, Vita was developing an unsympathetic and callous attitude towards me. She unfortunately dashed all my hopes that were pinned on her. She turned out to be a woman of perverted personality, trying to be in the good books of our in-laws by joining them in their malicious moves of torturing me both physically and mentally. Vita was a woman of Indian origin from Malaysia and had received her education in English public schools. She had lived in a society with no inhibitions, dressing and mixing with males freely, whereas I had my education in ordinary Indian schools and lived a life which was full of strictures regarding dress code and mixing with the opposite sex. Kadam's attitude and behaviour to me was very distressing and inappropriate. He wanted me to dress, joke and laugh like Vita but I was not brought up to be like her. Her limits of permissiveness were different from mine and I was proud to be the traditional one.

During my stay in Newcastle I was doing a lot of introspection. I remember not showing my true emotions to anyone. I avoided talking to my uncles and aunts, as I could not see anyone who could assist me and mitigate my sufferings. I wanted to spend all my time in planning my future course of action to come out of this messy situation. But everything was hazy and I had no choice but to go back to Liverpool and carry on with my life. I enjoyed being with my nephews. I received a lot of gifts, in cash and material, for my baby. When Manu dropped me back to Liverpool after a week at his home, my in-laws opened my bags and grabbed what I had brought from Newcastle, commenting that it was simply not enough. Their remarks and the atmosphere in the house choked me. One afternoon, only Kusha and I were at home. I had done all the housework. She was sitting, sunbathing, in the back garden. As I went out to sit with her, she said, "You know that people who leave their wives, can leave their kids too. Don't you ever think that this baby you are carrying is going to let you live in this house forever." It shocked me as there was no legitimate reason for her to say such a thing to me. I asked her what I had done to deserve this condemnation and she said that she was just making me aware of my situation with respect to the child I was carrying. I kept praying to God and hoped for a boy. Sawi and Dinki wrote beautiful letters to guide me to eat sensibly and keep warm.

I needed new clothes as my stomach grew during the later stages of my pregnancy. When I asked Sajan, he slapped me on my face and said, "Your brother has a clothing shop, why doesn't he send you some more clothes?" In this house, when anyone hit me, they expected me to carry on with my work straight afterwards without even giving me a chance to cry.

The weather was getting colder. One day, all of a sudden, Kadam gave me twenty pounds to keep and told me not to tell anyone. He also said he would give me more to buy a coat for myself. I kept the money in one of my handbags which Vita would use without my permission. She never asked me for my things. Whenever she wanted anything she would sneak into my room and help herself. She was in the habit of searching my bags without my permission. When I discovered that the twenty pounds were missing, I told everyone. They all shouted and accused me of hiding it or sending it to my brother. No one believed me. All I could do was talk to God and my baby listening inside me.

There was another miserable incident that winter. Everyone was going to a wedding. Nothing would fit me, so I couldn't attend it. Kadam let everyone else go and offered to keep me company. He played my wedding video and started drinking. I grew very emotional on seeing my family and I started crying. What happened next, I could not have imagined in my wildest of dreams. It was a nightmare for a brief moment. Consoling was the excuse he relied upon and suddenly his behaviour turned most inappropriate. Deep down, I felt like slapping and spitting at his face, but I pushed him away with all my strength and ran to my room and bolted it from inside. I sobbed and prayed for everybody to come home soon. When everyone returned I felt a sign of relief. No one would have believed me had I opened my mouth and exposed Kadam's true character. On the contrary, everyone would have assassinated my character with most slanderous remarks. Over eighteen years have now passed since that evening. I feel sick with the stink of that man, whenever that moment surfaces in my memory.

I debated in my mind whether I should narrate this disgusting incident to my family members. Fear of a drastic reaction made me remain silent. Moreover I did not want to add to the mental agony Manu was passing through because of me. I stayed away from Kadam and I did not look at him at all. Each time I wished him good morning to make it look normal to Sajan and Kusha, he would make a face and ignore me. Life got harder and harder. Kusha would make excuses to be angry with me so that Sajan ignored me for months during my pregnancy. Kadam would slap me as hard as he could in front of the family whenever he was drunk. They all would watch me get beaten without any feeling and would enjoy the sight as if it were an entertainment.

One day, coming back from the hospital on my own, I ran for the bus. I fell down in the middle of the road. I tore my dungarees and my knee was bleeding. I was a few days away from delivering my baby. Because I fell, I missed the bus and had to walk at least two miles to be home as quickly as possible. I came into the house and told Kusha about my fall, and was about to go up to change when she shouted at me, "First you come late, and now you're off to your room. Don't you know you have clothes to fold and iron?"

I replied, "Please let me change and see to my bleeding knee. It has been bleeding for some time. Then I will do as you say."

She pulled my hair and said, "Will your father, who has given you nothing, come from India to do this work? How dare you think of leaving it for later? How dare you speak like this in front of me?"

She phoned Kadam and asked him to come home from the shop and sort me out for speaking this way in front of her. He came in yelling at me, hit my face violently and asked me what my problem was. I explained, "I only asked Mum to let me go upstairs to change my clothes and clean my knee and she started shouting and has called you home." As soon as she heard that, Kusha pulled my hair and beat me up again, calling me a liar. Kadam told her to beat me as much as she wanted to and not to worry even if the baby died, as he would see to the consequences. He left Kusha to finish up beating me to see if I would lose the baby. I cannot remember when he left—Kusha was still slapping me. She gave me nothing to eat that day. I had to do without the leftovers. I sobbed all night with no one to comfort me. I had no communication with Sajan. He was basically a mother's baby from day one. I thought all night and prayed that I give birth to a baby boy. I decided I would give him to Dinki if my in-laws chucked us out. Knowing my sister Dinki's nature, I was sure that she would definitely have loved my child and given everything the baby needed. My baby would have a home, but I was so disgusted with life that I just did not want to live. Everyone in my in-laws' family was malicious and they looked for the flimsiest of excuses to beat me up.

10
One Hope

In life, one hope is always replaced by another. It was true in my case too. Soon I was totally focused on the new arrival, who might bring joy and relief and pull me out of this sense of hopelessness. I was also hoping against hope that the birth of a child might bring about a change in my husband, bringing him close to me, the mother of his child.

I had no one in Liverpool who could hear me out. I cried silently and constantly. I prayed to God incessantly to bless me with a baby boy because both of my sisters had daughters. I went to the temple to pray before the delivery. There I met an old lady who taught the teachings of Hinduism at Liverpool University. She was considered to be very noble and spiritual. She blessed me that I was going to have a baby boy and said I should call him 'Rohit'. The baby was ten days overdue. Everyone in Newcastle had been anxious to find out. They sent my younger brother Ballu, who had just arrived from India. Ballu came to see me a day before Rohit was born. I was thrilled to see him and to know that he would be there to share my happiness. For the last thirty-six hours, Ballu and I waited for the childbirth. He carried out the duty of accompanying me instead of my husband as if he were the father.

God heard my prayers and on 15 November 1986, I gave birth to a lovely baby boy. This time, I cried for a different reason. It was certainly the happiest day with the thought that, finally, one of us sisters had a boy. However, Kusha did not want me crying in front of the nurse. In the delivery room before she left, she swore and shouted at me for crying, and giving the wrong impression to the nurse. Little did Kusha know that crying has nothing to do with happiness or sorrow, it has only to do with extremes.

Ballu informed my family about my having a baby boy, as my in-laws did not bother to do so. Ballu went back to Newcastle the day after. I was dying for my sisters to come and see my baby. I received telegrams from my whole family in India.

I had been asking my in-laws and the rest of the family for a name, but they were unconcerned. The hospital was pressing for a name. I noticed that my baby's cot was the only one without a name on it. By the third day, the nurse asked me if I had thought of a name for my baby. The only name I had in mind at that time was Rohit, and I remembered the enigmatic lady from the temple and thanked her in my mind. The following day, when my in-laws saw the baby's name tag on his cot, they told me off for naming him and taking away their right to name him. I tried telling them that all the other babies in the ward had a name, so I gave a name to mine. If they did not like it, they could change it.

I stayed in the hospital for five more days with my son. I spoke to him all the time, telling him what I was going through. Now I had somebody to listen to me and understand. It felt wonderful to have someone who belonged to me. Rohit was mine. Funnily, Sajan brought a card. It said "It is a Boy" on the outside and "Congratulations on your baby boy" on the inside. I laughed when I looked at it and crossed out the letter "y" to make it "our". I still have that card. When I look at it now, I know it should have stayed in its original wording. I was naive to change it.

When I took the baby home, on the first night, Kusha ordered Sajan to sleep in a separate room. Rohit and I slept in my room that night. In that house, from the first night onwards, my baby belonged to a single parent. It hurt me a lot not to be able to share our baby and welcome him home together as other couples do.

The following week I was back in the hospital. For ten days, I was in the Intensive Care Unit as I had stiffened up after a small operation to make sure that there was no afterbirth left in me. Although Rohit was with me, I could not feed him or pick him up. No one informed my family of my re-admission. I had no moral support from anyone around me. They were all too busy to see my emotional state or notice the suffering.

Manu came to see the baby in early December. He was so happy to have a nephew that he brought much more in the shape of gold, cash, material and food, than any member of the community could expect. But my in-laws never spoke to him or offered him any food or drink. As usual they had expected a lot more than what came their way. Anyway, by this time I was used to hearing them demand money in straight words. Manu had to ask for some sugar from my mother-in-law, saying, "It is a tradition that I have a sweet from you to share the happiness on Rohit's arrival." Only on his request did she offer him a cube of sugar. He took one piece, blessed me and left. The happiness that I wanted to share with Manu evaporated because of the atmosphere. I wondered if the sugar did actually taste sweet to him. As soon as he had gone, I took myself up to my room and cried as I was unable to share my true feelings with him. I wished my heart would just stop beating. Manu left with pent-up emotions and I felt that he must be crying too. Later on I discovered that he really did cry for my ill fate.

A month after Rohit's birth, I had four wisdom teeth removed and I remember taking him to the clinic and back on my own. Rohit and I were in pain. He was crying as he must have been hungry. My mouth hurt and I must have been feeling drowsy from the injections.

When I reached home, Kusha was there while the others were at work. Nobody could see the pain that I was suffering. Kusha opened the door and the pram hit the door, making a loud noise. She slapped me for banging the door. She said that I had not brought this door in my dowry. I had therefore no right to bang it. I apologised and told her I was in pain. I cried the rest of the day.

When I look back, it is heartbreaking for me to remember the time I spent with my in-laws. There was no love or care for me. Being a loving person myself, I expected to be loved at least by Sajan. Kusha caused problem after problem between us, accusing me of doing things that I had not done and so Sajan drifted away. Maybe he was never there. Each time I made an effort to come close to him, she came in the way. After Rohit's birth, Sajan did not touch me or love me. He looked at me as if I was a doormat, a slave, a spare tyre. Holding this baby, I did not know where to go. I used to tell Rohit he was born in the wrong home, he should have been born in India in Dinki's house, where he would have been loved the most.

I was very worried. Life seemed to get more burdensome for me. I had no idea how to make it better for our future. Sajan's uncaring, thoughtless and ignorant behaviour was most hurtful. My energy to cope was running out fast — thoughts of running away or committing suicide were crossing my mind every now and then.

11
Depression

I suffered post-natal depression and was suffocating from within. My husband found no fascination in my body or soul. My mother-in-law always nagged and taunted me. Often finding faults with my appearance, she commented that I was dark complexioned, short structured and unattractive. My father-in-law had obviously a vindictive attitude towards me for foiling his incestuous advances towards me when I was alone at home. For my brother-in-law Bajiv, I was nothing more than a domestic help who could be slighted and ordered around. His wife, Vita, was an extrovert, which made her popular company among the liberal-minded. My Indian values ensured I was overshadowed by her towering ubiquitous presence. My parents expected me to settle in my in-laws' family, giving them no occasion and excuse for any complaint. Like most Indian parents, they wanted that after my marriage I should not be a source of any inconvenience for them. Although my brothers did a lot for me, they wanted to lead an undisturbed life themselves. Being an introvert, I did not have any friends with whom I could share my grief and lighten my heart. I had become simply an unprotected waif with nothing to feel proud of. When the sky of my life was overcast with such clouds, I felt like running away, as I could not take any more, and got angry at myself for living as I did.

One day, I was so desperate that I left Rohit and ran out of the house. But Vita brought me back from a few yards away. She called the doctor and told him that I was trying to escape. The health visitor was also called out and Vita explained everything to them, how I was treated like a slave. The doctor told me that he could not do anything as it was a family matter, unless I wanted to report the matter to the police. My first thought was for my parents and brothers and fears of the unknown. I told Vita and the doctor not to mention anything to my in-laws' as it would cause more problems for me. I promised them, there and then, that I would not run away again. As usual Vita took advantage of the situation and told my in-laws that I had tried to run away. She tried to prove that she only wanted to be loyal to them and that she had saved their reputation. Thanks to that, she gained their support in everything she wanted to do in that family. She played a double game to please both sides.

Kadam rang Manu to tell him that I felt inferior to Vita for not bringing as much as she had. In February, some of my in-laws' friends came and they were told by Kusha that I did not bring enough. She added that if it had been up to her, she would already have thrown me out. I called the health visitor and told her how insulted I felt in front of other people and that I could not take any more. She asked me to think about my life and the baby and leave if I could not cope with it. I considered the position I was in, thinking of all the housework, work at the shop, taking care of the baby both day and night. I could not muster enough strength to accept the health visitor's opinion. I was being used all the time in every way by everyone. Aunt Nirmal came to see me and the baby. She was insulted and sent back with a message to my rich parents to send more cash. My in-laws told her that they had found the wrong family for their son. In their view, I was an ill omen for their son's success in life.

One day, the midwife who used to come and visit me after Rohit's birth sent the social worker. The social worker brought a doctor to see me. He explained that I was going through post-natal depression. I told them how I was treated, how I was fed with the leftovers and stale food and expected to do all the housework and look after the baby. The social worker asked me why I did not go to Newcastle to see my family if I was not happy here.

At that time, Manu and Sanju were in India to shop for Ballu's wedding. Ballu had now been engaged to Chandni Syal for a few weeks. I needed help desperately for my mental and physical state, and I decided to visit Newcastle and tell them what exactly I was going through. I wanted my brothers to realise the facts of my life. I called my health visitor to show her the clothing and items I was taking with me, for Rohit and myself. I did not want anyone to accuse me of taking any more than I needed. I rang Sajan to inform him that Ballu needed me in Newcastle, so I was going there. I had not told anyone in Newcastle. I took a taxi without a penny and on arrival, I told Ballu to pay the driver. Seeing me heartbroken and sad, lonely and hard-up, Ballu got the shock of his life. He was too young to grasp my position.

Ballu informed Aunt Nirmal, who dreaded the thought of me, a married Indian girl, living alone with her baby, wanting a support network that no one could provide for her. They considered me as a social obligation dumped on them for no fault of theirs, as our Hindu society and its customs do not approve of a young married girl with a baby stepping out of her marital home. Basically what I wanted and needed was to leave my marital home, and find help from my parents, or my brothers. I no longer wanted to be where I was so shabbily treated. All those dreams of being married, having a husband, my own home, my children, wearing lovely clothes and jewellery, all the many little thoughts I had always had were broken and shattered dreams.

My brothers wanted me to do better, to be stronger and fight for my rights in Liverpool. How could I have done that?

I had tried to the very best of my abilities to survive and could not try any more. I had five people hating me constantly, making my life hell. How could I have survived? Anyway, everybody in Newcastle told me off for coming. They reasoned and asked me what the family would answer to society. What would people think? They talked about Rohit's future, and how he would need his father's support. This totally confused me.

My in-laws rang my brother, telling him to send me home so that they could keep a closer eye on me in future. In their opinion, I had run away with their baby. I did not want to go back at all, but Ballu could not keep me as it would affect his marriage. His family name would be slandered in society, if one of his sisters left her marital home in this way. Manu arrived back with materials for Ballu's wedding and found me there. He pitied himself for being so helpless. I did not have the power to change the situation, otherwise I would never have put him through all this heartache. My life became a huge question mark. Manu, hoping for a miracle, asked me to hang on.

12
Back in Hell

Once again it rained from Newcastle to Liverpool while Manu drove me home, along with Aunt Nirmal and Uncle Sehgal. Bajiv was at home but he would not allow any of us in the house until Kadam and Sajan arrived from work. We had to wait outside in the car for two hours. Rohit was tired and was crying after the long journey. His nappy was dirty and he needed a feed, so he couldn't be consoled. When I entered the house, Kadam swore at me and slapped me several times very hard, in front of everybody. I still remember how painful and hurt I was. I knew things would get even harder from now on because Manu was not going to be there very long. He was only there to drop me. He stood there mutely and watched me being beaten. He tried to explain the situation to me, that Kadam was angry, and now that I had a baby, things would settle in time. He also said that after Ballu's wedding, he would bring Mum and Dad to Liverpool. Before leaving, he said to me, 'You were Sita, from now on you should become Gita'. At the time I didn't understand what he meant. I later learned that in the Hindi movie, *'Sita aur Gita'*, Sita was a very humble, kind-hearted girl who was always taken advantage of by her scheming aunt. Gita was her separated twin, who was precisely the opposite. In the movie, the two girls meet and switch roles, Gita teaching a lesson to Sita's aunt and uncle. When I learned this, and realised what Manu had meant, I laughed to myself, thinking that this is easier said than done. A Hindu daughter is brought up to be a homely girl; her parents bring her up to become a Sita, not a Gita. It's harder than it sounds to switch roles.

Deep down in my heart, I knew that if I needed help again, I would not seek it from society. It would have to come from elsewhere, maybe from God. Kusha snatched Rohit from me and said I was not allowed to touch him for a month as punishment. Vita took advantage of the situation by holding Rohit, saying that from now on she would take care of him, using it as an excuse to make me do her work as well as my own. She called me a bitch whenever I walked past her, or whenever she needed to say something to me. It was almost as though I didn't have a name any more. In the shop, there was a small table next to the wall, with a mirror hanging above it. I recall Vita conveniently leaning over me, while I ate, to use the mirror and spray her hair spray, making a point of getting it in my food.

I used to sit on a seat in the middle of the shop when there were no customers about, keeping an eye on everything. Vita hung a note there for me, saying, 'All yours is mine, all mine is mine, you stupid BITCH!' I showed it to Kadam, and at first he laughed, then threw the note away. I strongly felt that it was their teamwork to drive me crazy and make me mentally disturbed.

My life became a drag. Looking at my son, I could not die. Rohit was the only person from whom I found the strength to fight, but I did not know for how long. I had always tried my best. I was not allowed to answer any phone calls, or make any. I was told in plain words, 'Do not touch the phone.' I had no one to talk to. I lost a lot of weight as I did not care for myself. My in-laws wanted to get rid of me. Whenever they would have friends visit the shop, they would discuss me, and make a point of doing so loud enough for me to hear. I remember once, Kadam's friend Bhandari said, "Just get rid of her, we will help your son get married again. This was a comment that left me in a state of fear, and sent shivers down my body wondering what was going to happen to Rohit and me.

Gradually, I noticed that my things were getting lost. I became confused. My jewellery, including Rohit's gold chain and my diamond wedding ring, went missing. Although everything was in Kusha's keeping, still I was accused of sending my jewellery to Newcastle. It hurt me a lot to lose the very chain and pendant that Manu had given to Rohit when he was born.

One night in June 1987, Kadam called me to his room, and in front of everyone asked me that if he was to hit me, what would I do. He slapped me six times on my face and told me to call Manu for help. I looked at Sajan, who pushed me and said that I deserved it. That night was another lonely night, as Kusha kept Rohit away from me. I spent it crying.

I went to Newcastle on *Rakshabandhan* a Hindu custom where brothers and sisters meet, the sister binding a ribbon on her brother's right wrist, reminding him that he is bound to her, and it is his duty to protect her. My in-laws sent me because both my family, and society, expected it. I was put on a freight train, as the seats on the train were cheaper, and Sajan was not prepared to pay much. I was sent to Newcastle, empty-handed and without a return ticket. I received a beautiful saree and boxes of sweets and chocolates as my gift for *Rakshabandhan* from Manu. Afterwards Manu came to drop me at the coach station to go back to Liverpool. I did not want to tell anyone in Newcastle of being beaten, as I knew it would cause more problems between Manu and my in-laws. My family was busy with the preparations for Ballu's marriage. I felt ashamed and guilty to ask Manu for the coach fare as I never received a penny from my in-laws. I could see the fire of mixed emotions, heartache, anguish and helplessness in his eyes when he gave me the money. If only I could have helped my situation, I would have never put Manu through this.

On the coach from Newcastle to Liverpool, alone with my baby, I waited longingly for my parents' arrival in England for Ballu's wedding and hoped for my survival.

13
Ballu's Wedding

My mum and dad arrived for the big day, in 1987, to attend the wedding and invited all of us. I was sent on my own with a message that Sajan would not go to a beggar's wedding. People in Newcastle had expected Sajan with me, as they had never seen him since we got married. On the wedding day, at least five hundred guests were waiting for Sajan to arrive. There is a traditional *milni* ceremony at Hindu weddings, where the girl's family meet their opposite members in the boy's family. Everyone had been welcomed and announced to the crowd and introduced to the bride's family. Everyone looked at me, questioning why Sajan was not there. People started gossiping, making me feel very nervous and tired of my situation.

My whole family was embarrassed for having to wait so long for Kadam and Sajan, who had been persuaded to come. My emotional state could be seen on my face as Sajan and Kadam came in late, almost at the end of the ceremony. They had never met my father before this event. Upon meeting him, Kadam continually asked him to step aside and talk about the money he was owed from my reception function, and demanded to know whether my father wanted to give more to his daughter, since he had not been present at her wedding. My father was forced to say that this function was neither the time, nor the place to discuss this problem, and that he himself would come to Liverpool to sort it all out.

I stayed in Newcastle till the completion of the wedding, with the newly-wed couple Ballu and Chandni. All the while I tried to keep a composed face in public. I had not been there for Manu's wedding and Ballu's was the last wedding in the family. I wanted to enjoy myself to my heart's content. I wanted to laugh, to dance and tell everybody how happy I was for a change. Sadly, I did not enjoy that day at all. Obviously, there was a deep-rooted happiness that this was my brother's wedding, whom I adored. But the smiles that I was forced to display at every instance, exhausted me mentally. Every time I smiled, I felt as though I was lying, both to the people I was smiling at, and to myself.

I placed the blame of Sajan and Kadam's behaviour on myself, feeling that somehow, I was the cause of all the disruptions during this supposed auspicious occasion. Both Manu and I knew that my parents' arrival in England was not going to rectify the situation I was in, and the expression on Manu's face when he looked at me, was one of sadness and disappointment.

Sajan and Kadam left before the wedding ceremony had finished, leaving me for a while to stay with my brothers. One week later, Manu was flying to Amsterdam for a holiday with one of his friends, and he phoned Virender, the friend who initially suggested that I should marry Sajan. Virender's wife told Manu that I had gone to hospital with Rohit, as he had been very ill. Manu came at once to find out what was wrong. Kusha came to the hospital and accused me of feeding Rohit bad food at the wedding, and not taking care of him properly, saying that I was a poor mother. She also accused me of calling Manu from the hospital, while I was there with Rohit, and asking him to come to Liverpool. There was no other way he could have found out. I left Rohit in the hospital crying, and ran after Kusha's car, pleading with her not to cause any more trouble, now that Rohit was ill. As she pulled away, I shouted at her, "Fine, do whatever you want to do, I don't care any more." Kusha, on hearing my remark, told

Sajan to call my father in Newcastle, and tell him that they were throwing me out, as they had no need for me any more. Dad was told to pick me up from the hospital, or outside their house, as I would not be allowed in. My father was shocked and pleaded with them to keep me for a few days, until he himself could come and discuss the matter. Rohit and I stayed in Whiston hospital for two days after he had recovered, because we had no home to go to.

On the 4th of September 1987, my twenty-third birthday, both my parents came to Liverpool in an attempt to sort things out. They brought with them gifts for everyone in the home, and *shagun,* i.e. money for everyone, as it was their first visit. My parents were not offered even a sip of water, or asked to sit down. My father enquired about the situation, and why I was being mistreated. Kadam's immediate answer was that they were treating me fine, and that I had an inferiority complex, as I had brought less dowry than Vita. My father, as humble as ever, holding his hands together, said that he had three daughters, and none of them had ever seen poor times. All of his daughters were given equal dowries, and Prerna had been given the best dowry out of all three, since she was the youngest daughter. My father said he couldn't believe that I had an inferiority complex, as I was the happiest of his five children.

On hearing my father's plea, and watching him lower himself to such levels, I couldn't remain silent about how I was being treated. I took my mother aside and told her that I was being beaten, but didn't have the courage to mention that Kadam had tried to molest me. My uncle Karamjeet Nayyar was with my parents, and my mother, who couldn't speak up in front of my in-laws, asked him to address them. He warned them that if I was being beaten, or mistreated, he would make sure there were dire consequences. I was relieved that someone had the courage to speak his feelings, which neither my father, nor my brother could do. As my parents were leaving, uncle Karamjeet Nayyar held Kadam's hand, as if to shake it, and quietly said to him, "If your hand touches our daughter again, rest assured, we know how to cut hands off." I overheard this comment, and feared that it may make the situation worse.

From that day, Sajan refused to speak to me, or even sleep in the same room as Rohit and me. I tried asking him many times, what my crime was, and what I had done wrong. His only answer was, "I don't want to talk to you, and you will know soon." Kadam used to taunt me, quoting his friend Bhandari's words, "Get rid of her, we will help your son get married again", as if he was planning to do so.

I knew deep down that there was no way for me to escape my in-laws. Society wouldn't help me, and my own family had tried, but failed to do so. Only God could help me now, and the quickest way out of that house, would be to take my own life. The only reason I did not, was Rohit.

14
God's Will

By the end of September, I was feeling very ill and exhausted both physically and mentally. My routine consisted of waking at around five in the morning and quietly dressing myself and Rohit, despite his protest at waking so early. I would check the house, and make sure everything was tidy and in its place, before leaving for the shop with Kadam or Sajan, as the milkman made his deliveries at seven. I would clean the shop as quickly as possible, sweeping and mopping it. I would stock all of the shelves, working till ten in the morning, when I was allowed to eat breakfast, accompanied by Vita's usual hairspray in my food. After a few minutes to eat, I would work in the shop. I was given the most undesirable jobs. I would have to clean the toilets two to three times a day. I would arrive home at around six in the evening, firstly taking care of Rohit, making sure he had all he needed, before cooking for everyone. I was not allowed to eat with them. I would eat what was left over, and clean all of the dishes. I would then put everyone's clothes in the wash, and take out the wash load from the day before, iron it, fold all the clothes, and place them in each person's individual rooms. I would sleep after everyone else, at around midnight, waking at least once during the night to feed and tend to Rohit.

I began shifting into an insomniac phase, where every minute was neither day nor night for me. I was constantly tired and feeling worse every day. As I became more and more exhausted, I pushed harder to complete all of my work, not wanting to give anyone a chance to shout at me. Painkillers were sold in the shop, and I was taking more than the usual dose, around twenty tablets of paracetamol a day, to no effect. I began having throbbing headaches throughout the day and night, and I had sharp pains in my neck. One night, I was in so much pain that Kadam himself was forced to call out a night doctor, as he did not want to have to wait in the emergency room, since I was crying hysterically. The doctor gave me some antibiotics, and said that I should see my general practitioner (GP) first thing in the morning. As he left, he said to Kadam, "I hope that this is tuberculosis, as the symptoms she has suggest a far worse illness."

Two weeks passed, and I was taking stronger medication. The end of September was approaching, and my health had rapidly deteriorated. One day at the shop, the pain in my neck was so bad, that throughout the day I constantly asked Sajan to take me to see the doctor again. It was almost closing time. Sajan hadn't given a second thought to my words. I shouted, "Please, take me to the hospital!" Kadam laughed, saying "Don't worry, we are about to close the shop. Having to spend two hours in the waiting room will soon make you feel better." Still, Sajan waited for closing time before taking me to the hospital.

I was checked by a doctor, who told me that I would have to see a specialist as soon as possible through my GP. The following morning at nine o'clock, Sajan took me to see the GP, who immediately referred me to an oncologist. Around half an hour later, I was seen by Doctor Tappin, who luckily was in his a clinic that morning. He held my hand and assured me that everything would turn out fine for me. He checked my neck, but his slightest touch was too painful

79

to bear. I broke down in tears, in front of Sajan. For the first time in a long while, someone had showed me some affection. Doctor Tappin assured me that if I waited in the hospital till he had seen all his patients, he would call another specialist, and have a biopsy done on my neck to determine the cause of the pain. He wanted to check if it was actually tuberculosis. I was given a bed, and told not to eat for eight hours. Sajan said that his time was precious and he was needed in the shop and warehouse, and left me almost as soon as I was told I had to stay the day. I lay alone, worried about Rohit, who was also alone at the shop.

That very night, as promised, a biopsy was conducted on my neck, under general anaesthesia. I woke a few hours later, and vomited violently, crying at the unbearable pain in my neck. Kadam came to the hospital, delivering a message that I had to get well soon, as the whole family was busy and no one had time to take care of my baby. I went home that night, as the thought of leaving Rohit alone any longer was unbearable.

Mum called me the next morning, and I told her about the preceding long twenty four hours, also informing her that I was suspected to have tuberculosis. My mother tried to comfort me, saying that I was fine and that I had gotten a scar on my neck for no reason. She said that the weather changes had probably given me a sore throat or a cold. I told her that after the biopsy, I had no headaches whatsoever, there was only the pain of the actual biopsy, which was comparatively less. I was saddened to think of my mother's situation, not knowing or being able to comprehend how much pain her daughter was going through.

I was not allowed to hold Rohit at work, as I would have to tend to all the customers. He used to be in his pram all the time, apart from when he cried. Even then, Vita would take him out and make me do her work as well. In the back of the shop, there was a room stocked with cans of food where Rohit was kept. One day, he fell out of the pram, hit his forehead on a can and had to have stitches on his forehead. No one seemed to realise how serious an injury this could have been for a nine-month-old infant, and I began to fear for Rohit, in addition to my own ill health.

I didn't know what the test results would show. Rohit had only seen the house and the shop since the day he was born. Sajan, Rohit and I had never been out as a family, and I wanted to go somewhere with him. I promised Sajan that I would tend to all of my work, and finish it early so we could go somewhere together, while giving him the excuse that it would be nice for Rohit after his injury. Sajan agreed for once.

Everyone in the house knew which evening we were going out. After a busy day, I wanted to shower before I went, as I had been cleaning the shop most of the day. When I reached the only bathroom in the house, Vita was inside. I knocked and waited three quarters of an hour outside. It was already after eight, the time we had set to leave, by the time Vita came out. When I went into the bathroom, I realised she had left the shower running, and had used up all the hot water.

I went downstairs, and calmly told Sajan that we would have to go another night, as I couldn't get dressed without having a shower. By the time I got ready, it would be time for Rohit to sleep. Sajan was almost in a rage, shouting furiously at me that I had wasted his time. He ordered me to get dressed and get ready to go, whether I had a shower or not. At my refusal, he slapped me repeatedly.

Kadam, in a sympathetic mood for a change, calmed Sajan down, assuring him that there would be hot water for me tomorrow, and we could go then. He scolded Vita for doing what she did, but she simply smiled, and went into her room. Kadam said to Sajan that there was no point in shouting at me, and ruining his mood for the night, and then took him downstairs to have dinner. I heard Rohit crying behind me, and shouted at Sajan to come back. Something came over me, and I don't know how or why, but I slapped

81

Rohit across the face in front of Sajan. I had never seen such anger on his face, and he began shouting, questioning why I had hit his child. I told him that I wanted to see if he would get upset at seeing his own child hurt. I then asked him, that if he could get upset over a nine-month-old baby, whom he never seemed to give a second thought to, what would the parents of a twenty-three-year-old girl feel, when they hear that she is being abused every day?

Sajan put Rohit aside and began slapping me furiously and repeatedly across the face. Kadam heard my screams and stopped Sajan. Kadam was shocked to hear that I had hit Rohit. Even after telling him why I did it, I wasn't allowed to touch Rohit that night. I cried myself to sleep, thinking that I had hurt my only child, taking out the anger I felt towards everyone else, on the one person that gave me strength.

The following evening, Kadam made sure that I went out, wanting Sajan to spend time with his child, and wanting society to see that we were a normal, happy couple. For me, that evening held no meaning but a painful reminder of the events that had transpired the previous night. Sajan was cold towards me throughout the night, barely speaking to me.

The following morning, I had an appointment with Doctor Tappin to find out the results of the biopsy. After what had happened over the last few days, I was almost praying that I did have tuberculosis. I thought that it might get me out of that house for a few days. Kadam and Sajan had made it obvious that Rohit was theirs, and that he could be taken away from me whenever they saw fit. I was thus no longer concerned about what the result would be. I heard a nurse calling Sajan and me in. The three doctors and the nurse were very soft-spoken and gentle. One doctor took my hand and asked me how I felt. He remarked on how elegant I looked.

At this treatment, I knew deep down that something was seriously wrong. Sajan was chatting casually with the doctors, who were reluctant to talk back. He asked what the biopsy had shown, and one of the specialists said that the lumps in my neck were much smaller than the ones that would be present if I had tuberculosis. I didn't understand many of the words that were exchanged, as they were all technical medical terms. Doctor Tappin told Sajan that I had Non-Hodg-kins Lymphoma, a form of cancer, and one of the worst kinds possible. He assured us that it responds well to treatment. He told me that I would be having chemotherapy, which had terrible side effects. He said that I would put on weight, and most likely lose my hair. He said that chemotherapy is known for killing any virulent cells present, but alongside, it also kills any good cells that may be present.

Childlike, I didn't grasp the meaning of what was being said. I jokingly said that if taking the treatment meant losing my hair, I wasn't taking it. Doctor Tappin looked at me, as if he could see through me, calmly saying, "If you don't take this treatment, Prerna, you have three months to live. If you're lucky." I smiled at him and thought, 'Who wants to live anyway?'

15
Help at Last

I felt that all was dark and hopeless and my road of life had come to an end. Cancer, a small lump in my neck, a lump of death was all that I could see. Everything else in the world stood still and silent. Darkness became the whole universe for me. It was an answer to my prayers; my eyes went everywhere, within and outside of me to look. I then smiled and felt that this was God's way of answering my prayers for deliverance. No doubt it was God's will for me to die of cancer instead of stooping or begging for life from others. I blushed and somehow thanked the Lord for answering my prayers so fast. I wished that my baby Rohit had never been born, as I had nothing to offer him but a bed of thorns. I remember wishing good things for him.

I wanted to see my family, to stay with my mother for the last three months. I did not want any treatment, I did not want to live any more. I did not want anything from the world. I had had enough. My mum and dad were in Newcastle with my brothers. I asked Sajan to inform them. He shouted at me in front of the doctor, saying that he had no wish to ring 'those beggars

The junior doctor advised Sajan to ring my parents as it was important for me. He rang Kadam and told him that I had cancer. When I heard the word in his voice, I lost my cool composure. I was sobbing. The nurse was holding on to me. I was telling her that I did not want to live. "Who wants to live?" I repeated, over and over. "God has heard me." She explained that it was a killer disease and that if I did not take any treatment, I would only last three months and my baby would not have a mother. The doctor made Sajan ring my family. He decided to ring Ballu at work rather than my father or Manu, to save himself from any probing questions. He dialled the number, using the hospital phone, and when Ballu answered the phone, he said, "Your sister has cancer" and put the phone down.

I hoped that the detection of this disease might change my in-laws' attitude towards me. I was hoping for feelings of kindness, mercy and affection, any show of humanity towards me, but alas, they had other ideas for me. Instead of getting me treated, they planned to force me out of the house and make me get myself treated either by my family or by someone in the society. They wanted me out, anywhere in the world but their home. They could not bear my presence at all. This dimension of their character had surfaced sooner than expected. Even though I had been given this diagnosis, Kusha said that I would have to continue my duties as usual, except for the days when I would have my treatments.

By this time, I had adopted a philosophical attitude towards life; I looked upon my approaching death as a blessing in disguise. I felt that sweet are the ways of adversity as it provides us many revelations which otherwise remain hidden, revelations of people's attitude and their unmasked faces, which perturbed me deeply.

The same day, when Ballu gave the news of my illness to my family, Manu and my mother came to see me at Liverpool. They both cried, holding on to me. My mother held me tight. It is ironic how people react to what they see with their own eyes. I remember my mother's reactions, when I told her about the biopsy. I could see her heart bleeding for me. If I was dying slowly of mental and physical torture, it did not matter so much to society. But dying with cancer brought everyone in our family to my rescue.

85

Manu held my hand and said, "You can't die. I won't let you." I smiled, calmly replying, "Who is afraid? I don't want to live and I am not frightened of death." He said, "I'm glad you are not afraid, because I am not going to let you die. Even if I have to take you to the ends of the earth for the treatment, I will."

I could see love in his eyes as he took leave of me and returned to Newcastle. My mother and I were given the spare room to sleep in. She held me tight against her as if I were a newborn baby. She stayed awake watching me all night. I was receiving all the attention that I needed from my mother. She kept on watching me, feeling me and making sure I was breathing. She tried to tell me that there was an effective treatment. Since I was in a developed country where the best of treatment was available, I would be all right. I could hear her pray for me.

The following morning, when my mother and I sat in the kitchen, Kadam asked my Mother if someone could help look after the baby and me, as all their family had to see to the work in the shop and at home. They could not spare any of their time for me or my baby. My mum rang Newcastle for my brothers to come and help. Manu came immediately bringing Ballu as my nurse. My mother and Ballu agreed to stay in Liverpool to look after me. Manu went back to Newcastle, as it was thought that if my brothers alternated their stay with me, one of them could tend to the family at home as well. My in-laws went on with their normal routine, totally indifferent to Mum and me. For them we did not exist. They were sure that I would die now. No one bothered to spare even five minutes to ask if I was feeling any better. My mother did the cooking, washing and cleaning and looked after Rohit as well. Sajan was already sleeping separately and acted as if he was busy all the time. My mother stayed for fourteen days. Kusha and Kadam approached my mother, telling her, "You didn't let your daughter live in peace by giving her what she needed in life. At least, let her die in peace. After all, she has got cancer. Firstly, she won t survive, and even if she does, we won't have her, so just leave, and let her die."

My mother's response was perhaps the most assertive one I have ever seen her make. She spoke in her normal voice, but with a power that I did not know she possessed. She said to Kadam, "We're both in our fifties; if we can't contemplate our deaths yet, how can I leave my daughter, of twenty-three alone to die, because you think she will?".

Kusha, in her usual tone, angered at my mother's confidence, said to her, "You can't stay here and get your daughter treated. We can no longer bear the burden of having you in this home. If you want her treated, you take her away and if she survives, get her married elsewhere as we will get our son remarried anyway. Your daughter has cancer now, and it's not good for Sajan to run after her to the hospital every day. She is of no use to us." Kusha also instructed my mother to take care of Rohit as she could not carry him and said that Rohit was too heavy.

My mother and I sat there. My mother was in a state of shock. I was glad in a sense that my mother had stood up for me. Deep down, after seeing my own family's reaction to my illness, I knew that I would be all right.

My family complied with Kadam's order that no one in our society should learn of this illness. Kadam agreed to help Manu find a house, in which he could keep me and have me treated. Manu, of course, was expected to pay for all of my needs. In a sense, it was better for Mum that no one found out. It saved her and my brothers from answering society's questions at a time that was difficult enough already. Even my father did not know of what was going on at this point. Whenever someone asked after me, my in-laws made pathetic excuses, telling them that I had a cold, or was too tired to come along with them. They wanted to be rid of me quietly so that Sajan wouldn't face any difficulties in remarrying. My mother also made excuses, not wanting her own family to find out for fear of what they might do. She said that I had complications after Rohit's birth, and she was taking care of me.

As far as my own point of view goes, in those days I don't feel I understood, or wanted to understand, anyone else's problems. It was sickening to me, the way in which everyone would lie, in a vain attempt to keep my condition a secret. Luckily for me, by now, both of my brothers were successful businessmen, and could just about afford to keep me, and have me treated, even if the treatment was against my wishes.

16
Just Ward 13

I spent my last moments at home, before my admission to hospital, with Rohit. I feel that he sensed I was going away, and was hence crying inconsolably. In these moments I felt a lot of change in myself. I began to see Rohit as a reason for living, and in an attempt to quieten him, told him so. He began to smile, reinforcing the view that I would have to fight this illness for him and recover completely.

At the time of my admittance, Kadam told Manu to hire a property closer to the hospital, so that, no one in his home would be disturbed. I went for a complete check-up, blood tests, a spinal test and a body scan, to make sure that the cancer had not spread any further in my body. My mother would sit beside me when I was at home. We never actually talked, but I don't think that we needed to vocally express our feelings, we each knew what the other was thinking.

I missed my tape recorder and my collection of ghazals, or melodic poems, by Mehdi Hasan, Ghulam Ali, Jagjit Singh and Bhupinder. One couplet that stayed in my mind was:

Lamhon ne khata ki thi,

Sadiyon ne saza pai.

Gam na kar

Zindagi pari hai aabhi.

The literal translation of which would be, the mistakes of a moment carry an eternal price, but do not feel sad, you still have a lot of life ahead of you. I found a great deal of truth in these words. I had made one major mistake in a moment, namely marrying to satisfy my own family and I knew that for this mistake, I would have to pay for the rest of my life, the duration of which was uncertain. I would often laugh at my own situation, and the cards that I had been dealt in life.

I had a lumbar puncture test, to check my bone marrow which was the most excruciating pain I had ever been through. The doctors explained to my mother that I was lucky that my cancer was detected in time. As it was Non-Hodgkin's Lymphoma, and a very aggressive type, I would survive if chemotherapy suited me. I would have to be kept in a very clean and hygienic environment. Although I would lose my hair, it would grow back. At that time I felt very strongly that I ended up with cancer because Sajan's family gave me such a hard time. Doctor Tappin warned me to keep away from anyone who had flu or viral infection because if I caught a cold, it could be fatal for me.

Doctors put a hygmin line through my heart for the treatment. I started to take antibiotics and some other medicines. I was getting used to the staff in my ward as I was hospitalised for sixteen days, undergoing a complete check-up before they could start with chemotherapy. I knew deep down that after I left the hospital, I would not have a home, marriage, status, anything I could call mine. I could hear my in-laws' words constantly ringing in my ears while I lay silently in this ward. My mother sat beside me daily. My in-laws had told her to take me away as they did not want to have anything to do with me or my treatment because I had cancer.

The nights were different, dark and frightening. I could see my problems in their true colours and illuminated at night. The nurses were kind; I could talk and cry in front of them rather than in front of my family. One of them came to know me right through and understood me completely. She knew what I meant when I spoke. In the dark I saw the real me and in the day others judged me according to their own parameters.

On the 15th of September, they explained that I would receive twelve sessions of treatment, one every week, for the next three months. They also gave me my first chemotherapy treatment that day. It tasted like poison. I was sick for five days. Ballu sat on the floor cleaning my vomit again and again. Ballu, my younger brother, was a perfect angel. He was my nurse and did a great job. I was grateful to God for blessing me with such a brother.

I was peaceful, knowing that my ordeal at Sajan's house was over, as they had made it abundantly clear, that if I did survive, their house would no longer be my home. I'm not sure what gave me peace in those days, perhaps it was that I had escaped, or perhaps it was that I didn't know if I was going to survive. I was glad that no matter what happened, my mother was beside me throughout.

My mum knew what I had been through without me having to explain every incident, it was as if she could read my mind. I still had not told her about my ordeal with Kadam's misconduct. I was not strong enough to face that issue, and I felt that all through my life, I would never be strong enough to counter the mental agony that he put me through. I did not tell my mother, and I knew that if my mother found out, it would not remain between the two of us. Regardless, I was glad to be with her, and the atmosphere in the hospital was the most restful and peaceful that I had experienced for a long time.

One night I remember telling a nurse about my losses in life. She could see my fear, knowing that in three days, when my current session of treatment was over, I would have no home to go to. I knew that I was homeless, no one's home or rented place would ever become my home. I had lost mine through my in-laws. They had abandoned a traditionally brought up girl, who had never been never taught to stand up and express her suffering, leave alone fight for justice.

91

As I was crying I realised that the nurse had sat beside throughout the night, listening to me. At last, before she got up to see to her other patients, she held my hand and offered me a room in her own house where she lived alone. It meant the world to me to know that she cared. As she left I went back to my own dark shell, trying to sleep. I covered myself until the morning, when Mum came. All fears and problems looked different in the daylight. The cover was still on me, covering my deepest thoughts and inner voices of the night before. I recognised through my own experiences, and the empathy and kindness I received from those around me, that I had to find a solution to all my problems by myself.

While Manu was desperately looking for a very clean accommodation, Sajan visited me for not more than five minutes every evening during my stay in the hospital. So did Kadam. They did not want the doctors or medical staff to find out the state of our marriage. The consultants asked me about my life history for their own records. I, not knowing how long I had to live, explained everything – how I was treated as a slave by my in-laws and about Sajan not loving or caring for me.

The following day, Doctor Tappin got hold of Sajan and asked, "Would it not be better if you could live with your wife and child separately?" He told the doctor that it was not allowed in Indian culture as men do not leave their parents after marriage. That made me laugh as it is not true. The doctor left and Sajan knew that I had explained my past history to the doctor. Sajan started to ignore and insult me more. He told me I should never have told anything to the doctor. I felt sorry for him although I kept silent.

Kadam was helping Manu in finding a place for me to move into. I realised that it was up to Mum and Manu to carry on my treatment. Somehow, I did not want to put my family through this. Manu found it practical not to waste time as the doctors had already started my treatment in Liverpool, therefore he wanted me to stay in a rented accommodation. Manu had been encouraged to do all that he could for me. Kadam's vicious mind wanted to see how far Manu would go to have me treated, little realising that I was the whole universe for Manu and Ballu, who never cared for the glitter of gold. Nurses gave me my medication and a box full of syringes and injections with a list of instructions, as they said I no longer needed to remain in hospital. I was taking about thirty tablets a day and I had to flush the hygmin line twice a day with an injection. That was a tricky thing to do because it is vital to inject without letting the air in. So after my first treatment, Sajan took my mother and me to his home. My mother had to supply the food for me. Although they had the grocery business, they would not even bring me a bottle of milk or a slice of bread. It was very hurtful. Sajan could have at least done that much for me. But he did not. I used to love Quavers crisps, and one day I had a strong craving and asked Kadam for some from the shop. He said, "It's easy for you to sit in bed and order what you like for free. We can't tend to your every need."

From that day onwards, I stopped eating Quavers. Now I eat better snacks than Quavers.

The question on everyone's mind was, would I survive, or would I die?

17
Chemotherapy

My entire family wanted to visit me and it was best for my in-laws to let me out of the house with my mum, as they did not want to meet anyone. Manu rented a beautiful, fully-furnished, three-bedroom bungalow in Park Road, Liverpool. It was very expensive for him so I was worried about the costs he may have to incur. Ballu nursed me. Sanju and Chandni took turns every week to stay with us. Ballu and Chandni had been married for just two months. Chandni and I had not had much of interaction, but now I saw her properly – a small, thin, very attractive young lady with dark, long hair reaching her hips and big brown eyes, running around working all day, always very elegantly dressed. My dad was told that I had cancer but I do not think he was in a state of mind to really know what was happening. The shock had made him dumbfounded. He was so flabbergasted. He came to see me and I felt that if I were to die now, I would have no complaints as I had my parents around me and I was at peace with the world.

From now on, my in-laws asked my parents not to bother them any more with my treatment. The hospital provided it free, and they were too busy to run after me. The arrangement was that Sajan would pick me up in the evening from the bungalow to take me home to be with him and Rohit, and he would drop me back at 7 a.m. the following morning. My mother used to look after me and made sure that I had my medication and care on time, and according to the doctors' advice. I felt it was a heavy burden on her. She was not sleeping at all. The medicines I took were very strong and made me very hungry at night.

One night, I asked Kusha for some food and she shouted rudely that there was nothing more for me to eat. She asked me to eat before coming or ensure that my mother prepared some food for me to bring with me to their house. I was really in pain and felt sick all night. Kusha left Rohit on my bed when he cried and said that her arms had elongated with Rohit's weight. I have known so many mothers-in-law in my life, but she is the first one who complained about the good health of her grandson. I told Sajan that if I survived, I would not want to live with Kusha as she kept telling me how heavy Rohit was.

Sajan stopped taking me to his house to be with Rohit, and explained that as I got hungry at night, it would be better if I was with my mum. After the third chemotherapy session, I started to lose my hair and when I looked in the mirror, I could barely recognise myself. Even the slightest noise gave me palpitations. My eyes were getting weak and I could not walk without support. I had to have injections to stop my vomiting. I became very sick. Anyone who goes through chemotherapy does not sleep at all, so I was awake during my treatment due to the medication, I think. Moreover, I missed my baby. I told the doctors and the nurses how fed up I felt. "I can't see my baby. They won't show me my baby." Out of frustration, Doctor Tappin told Sajan that he needed to take better care of me, and let me see my child. My mother rang Kadam, requesting him to show Rohit to me.

My mother received a phone call from Kadam, telling her to keep me with her from now on. The excuse was that someone had a cold in the house and they did not want me to catch it. My mother struggled through the rest of the week to keep me going and kept ringing my in-laws, asking them if I could go home. I should have been with my son and I had no clothes either. My mother kept on ringing for my necessities and they kept on making false promises, but no one ever took me home or brought anything for me. The only clothes that fitted me were two nightdresses and a jogging suit.

My future seemed bleak to me. When Chandni took me to the hospital for my next treatment, I refused to take it. The nurse made me sign a sort of disclaimer form that I was responsible if anything happened to me. I came home and sat down quietly. Chandni told my mother about this. My mother was helpless. She rang my in-laws for help, to take me back to hospital for the treatment. She wanted Sajan to assure me that he would take me back after the treatment, but my in-laws simply told her not to ring them ever again as they were not a taxi service.

I thought that no one, no one at all seemed to be so important for me to go through all this pain and this miserable treatment. Sajan could take care of our baby. Even if I did survive, what would my mother do with me? I had no future, no home, no life, no status. Now that I looked ugly as well, I thought that if people did not love me when I had the good looks and beautiful hair, how could Sajan accept me the way I was now? I was fat, dark and I carried a label on my forehead, 'Cancer Patient'. If I survived, who would bring me to hospital for further treatment when my mother went back to India?'

My mum sat on the floor, touched my feet and said she wanted me to continue with the treatment. I couldn't see her like this, so I gave in and went back to the hospital with Chandni. I sat down when the nurse came with my injection for my chemotherapy. I told her I did not want it and would not take it. I remembered having a lot of hysterical attacks. I cried and told the nurse that I would not have any more treatment. So she agreed and asked me once again to sign a discharge form. She sat me down and tried to calm me.

Chandni was telling me off for not taking the treatment. Then she tried her best to persuade me, pleading, "Please, please, take the treatment or what will I tell Mum when I go home? Why will you not take the treatment?" She tried to reassure me. In fact, her own twelve-year-old sister had died from cancer. She could not bear to lose another dear one to cancer.

Chandni developed a special bond with me, and as she watched me going through chemotherapy, she would remember her sister. She used to tell me how much her sister suffered but still did not survive. She also tried telling me that I was responding to the treatment, whereas her sister had rejected the treatment completely. I was made aware that chemotherapy was the only thing one could undergo for cancer. If you responded to the treatment you would be alright and live a bit longer; you had hope. She got me to agree to take chemotherapy.

In my case, this treatment was the worst thing going into my body and making me sick. Survival was more sickening to me, than the future I expected. Even the sight of the tablets I took made me sick. I started taking tablets every morning at 5 a.m. and finished at midnight. They were a mixture of antibiotics, steroids and God knows what else. Medically, I cannot tell what treatment I had but it was like going through hell. I would be constantly sick on the days when I underwent chemotherapy, which was every Wednesday. I would be sick until Friday, and by the following Tuesday, I would start to feel a little better, before my next treatment on Wednesday. I had to have more injections to stop the sickness and then I would all of a sudden be so hungry that I would want to eat everything. I had these funny cravings for different foods because at the back of my mind, I was not sure how long I would live. Anytime I wanted any particular food, I wanted it instantly because there was no surety that I would survive till tomorrow.

By now, I missed all the people I had ever met in my life. Each time I closed my eyes, I would see their faces. I wanted

97

everyone to visit me but sadly, no one knew I was suffering from cancer because Kadam had stopped us from telling others. My parents still hoped that I would go back with Sajan, that is why they did nothing against Kadam's will. Kadam was very clever and my parents were unaware of his plans.

Uncertainty stared me in the face all the time. Sajan was just not there; there was no help whatsoever from my in-laws. No financial or emotional support was provided by them. I did not exist as far as they were concerned. They still had not let me see my baby. I was heartbroken. At the back of my mind I felt that my baby must be missing me. I was counting the days since Rohit and I had seen each other. Sanju and Chandni comforted me all they could.

Weeks turned into months. I was with my mum, and my dad was very depressed. He came after hearing about my illness, but he took to excessive drink. I think he needed to drink to forget his sorrows. Manu had rung Billa in India to tell them that I had cancer. Billa rang Manu regularly till he was sure that I would pull through. Only then did he tell Dinki about it. Dinki and my nieces prayed day and night for my recovery. I received many letters from them. I was truly loved by them. Their prayers did bring a glimmer of hope to me at times.

Sawi was not informed due to her own problems in life. I wondered about the future of both of us, and its effect on my parents and family. We were all oscillating between hope and despair.

18

Doctor Tappin

Infused with a missionary spirit, humanitarian consideration and devotion to their profession, the medical staff kept fighting diseases to the last. There may be only a one per cent chance of a patient's survival, yet with a sense of optimism, they try to make the best of that, hoping to multiply it a hundred times. The oncologist Doctor J.A. Tappin, under whose treatment I was, possessed a high sense of devotion to his profession and was a great man at heart. He left no stone unturned to bring me back to my normal life by treating this killer disease. My present life owes its existence to that angel only. The expenses to be borne for the treatment of this disease are usually exorbitant. The realisation of this fact and the remote chances of the cure of this disease and the excruciating pain that the treatment involves, leaves little desire in a patient to live any more. To save a patient from all these complexities, the doctor has to play a great role. He has to not only cure his patients physically, but also has to treat them psychologically by boosting their morale and creating in them the will to live. Dr. J.A. Tappin wonderfully achieved these in my case.

I constantly thought whom I could live for. What was my future? Again, my mother saw me come back too quickly from the hospital. She knew I hadn't had my treatment, and told me off, almost in tears herself. I was taken back to the hospital by my mother. She caught hold of me and said, "You will live for your son and for your parents. You have us."

Dr Tappin was called out of his clinic and told that I was being fussy and not taking my treatment. He came to the ward especially for me. I remember clearly; I was sitting in a chair. He was the top oncologist of that hospital. He was very well known but there he was, on the floor, holding my hand as I was crying. He took a tissue, cleaned my nose, and said, "Look, just look at the things you make me do. The patients are sitting and waiting for me in my clinic and I am sitting here, cleaning your nose." He gave me an example of the a ship rocking in the storm of my cancer and said that he was the captain and I had to help him by taking the treatment to save the ship. He had to take the ship from one end to the other without sinking in the storm, without killing my parents and son on board. I was the ship, cancer was the storm, the doctor was the captain, and my family was on board.

He was not going to let go of me just by my signing a form saying that I did not want the treatment. I was his youngest patient at that time in the ward. All the other patients were seventy to eighty years old, dying with cancer but I was only twenty-three. He persuaded me. I cried uncontrollably. He sat there until I agreed to take the treatment because he was not going to let me go without it. He was determined to give me the treatment, and I had no choice but to give in. He was more powerful than I was, physically and mentally.

The attitude of Indian and English cultures towards me has been so different. I am so lucky to have had the help of GPs, consultants and the hospital staff. I have never ever been neglected in this area of my life. I have been given preference for any appointment whenever I needed it, and I have always felt comfortable with the arrangements. It must be difficult for those who do not get their appointments on time. There are patients who do not get the right doctor at the right time, but in my case I thank God for all the doctors, all the medical people involved who helped me out. They gave me my life back, to help my son, to be able to see him grow and enjoy his company.

I realised that my mother was going through so much already. She basically had come to England with my dad to attend Ballu's wedding and had ended up with me and my illness. She was staying in this country because of me. My brothers came every weekend to see my progress. My sisters-in-law were still taking turns to give Mum a hand in looking after me. Thinking of these and all the money Manu was spending to keep me alive, I knew I could not give in. There was Rohit. I knew if I did not fight, no one would look after Rohit and young as he was, he would not be able to face the vagaries of life and the cruelties of my in-laws. All this made me more determined than ever to pull myself out of this disease. So from that day onwards, I took the treatment for others rather than for myself.

To save a cancer patient, other than the indispensable doctor, the dear and near ones of the patient also have a very vital role. That vital role can be played only by unselfish people, who take the time to see what is in the patient's interests. I was fortunate on this account. During this period, I realised the wonderful and godly qualities Manu had. Earlier, during my marriage also, he had behaved not just like a brother but also played the role of my father with great responsibility and magnanimity. During my treatment he again repeated the past role. Rare are such caring and sacrificing brothers. I found him exceedingly mature, carrying a wise head on his young shoulders at the tender age of twenty-seven. He showed such profundity, nobility, and magnanimity that it is hard to find a comparable peer in this world. I owe my treatment, survival and existence mainly to him.

What I would wear, eat, and where I would live after my treatment, was always on my mind.

19
Challenges before a Cancer Patient

Doctor Tappin would provide wigs to all of the patients in his ward, paying for them himself. He used to hire a wig company, who would specially make them. They took a sample of my hair with them, and brought me five or six wigs, in different styles. I was highly impressed with both Doctor Tappin's generosity, and the quality of the company he had chosen.

The wig gave me a new look and an insight into the fact that looks can be deceiving, and can be taken for granted. Sajan would not even bring me a nightdress, or other necessities like clothes, shoes and a tape recorder, even though I had all of my possessions a mile away, in his home. My mum had to provide everything, relying heavily on Manu. It was so cold. I was weak, frail and felt the chill of winter even more, but still, they would not give me my coat or my boots. I remember the total amount of money I had with me was £60. I took Chandni to town and bought her the shoes she wanted. It was the first time I had bought a gift for her. And we only had a pound left to take the bus back. I was glad that I had taken this opportunity to buy her something, not knowing if I would have another opportunity in the future. Now I realise that the human mind normally takes life and its opportunities for granted.

Although I did not need the money at that time, I wondered who would provide for me because I am not the type to ask others for anything. It hurt me so much not having my clothes with me. I had wardrobes full of clothes at my in-laws' but they just would not give them to me. It was torture. My family persuaded me that if I have a life, I have everything, perhaps not realising what it means to have your personal possessions. They told me to fight for life first and continue the treatment. "We will get you more clothes." I could not express the feelings and sentiments I had for the things my in-laws had kept. Material bought for a daughter or a sister as a gift is a blessing. Taking the same gift in times of crisis and need is not the same and feels more like receiving charity.

I was getting fatter because of the steroids. The only night dress I had and the couple of suits my mother had given me were getting tighter. I remember Manu got me a coat and one outfit to go to the hospital. I wore the old suits at home and this new outfit for every visit to hospital. My body became weaker and weaker every day. I could not walk at all, I felt dizzy and had palpitations. Even someone breathing next to me or the slightest noise sounded so loud that it irritated me. I was sick. Still I had not seen my baby.

Throughout my treatment, I felt loved by everyone around me, especially my own family. Still however, I felt hollow inside, as the two people I wanted by my side were Sajan and Rohit. Nevertheless I carried on with my treatment.

After the sixth treatment, my weakness increased. Sanju, Chandni and Mum gave me all the help they could. They had to hold me and accompany me everywhere, even to the toilet. I could not open my eyes for very long. My finger nails turned black, my gums changed colour, my whole face felt bloated. In a matter of six weeks, I looked and felt like a seventy-year-old. I used to collect all my hair that fell on my bed; I had a bag full of it. I used to laugh and say that I wanted this bag insured as it was my hair.

At the end of eight sessions of treatment, it had been nearly two months since I had seen my baby. I told Dr Tappin that I was forbidden to tell anybody what was going on. On the one hand I was dying, on the other I was stopped from talking about it. I told him that they were not showing me my baby. So he himself rang and asked Kadam to bring Rohit over to me.

The nurses too rang a few times, and then Vita brought Rohit to the hospital just for a few hours on the day of my treatment. The relief I felt when I saw Rohit was overpowering. I felt like a thirsty person who sees a well for the first time. He had not forgotten me although I had lost my hair and looked different. I picked him up and started playing with him like I always did. People around me in the ward saw him and one of the patients said, "This is it. He is your dynamite. He is your strength, nothing will happen to you, you will survive and will be fine." And the word dynamite meant a lot to me. Rohit only stayed for an hour. I did not know when I would see him next.

A cancer patient has to face a multitude of challenges on different fronts. Not only does he or she suffer from excruciating physical pain but is also psychologically shattered. Many times, the reactions of different people add to the psychological complexities and crises of the patient. Some orthodox and superstitious people consider it an ill-omen to sit near the cancer patient – the 'evil spirits' present in the body of the cancer patient may make them its victims also. The ignorant and unlettered look upon it as an infectious and contagious disease. For them, to sit near the cancer patient can expose them to the dangers of contracting the disease like the plague. Many are eager to see and study the physical and psychological changes visible in the cancer patient. Persons with spiritual leanings and the spirit of service show a different kind of attitude. They take pride in providing a cancer patient with physical and psychological relief. They look upon it as a God-given opportunity to do a noble deed and a good turn by serving a cancer patient.

20
Rohit

It was Rohit's first birthday. I had so many dreams for this day. I took a taxi and went to Sajan's house to be with Rohit. I was not frightened of catching anyone's cold. I felt I may not be here for his second birthday. The thought of my baby losing me was frightening. Everyone made me feel that it was a pity I had cancer and it was Rohit's bad luck on his birthday not to have a grand celebration. Their feelings were not right but still somehow I felt very happy to be around on his birthday. I wanted a hug from Sajan and thought maybe he would say to me, "Congratulations, it is our son's first birthday!" But he did not. I thanked God for being there for Rohit. I was dropped back at night to be with my mum with the message that Kadam had a cold and a cough and I had a chance of catching the infection, and as the doctors did not recommend any of that, I should keep away. They somehow had good excuses to keep me away from Rohit and how I was to change that, only God knew the answer. Did no one know the feelings in a mother's heart on her child's first birthday? I knew I could not be with him at night because of my illness but my heart flew out to him to hug and bless him.

From then on we kept on ringing, "Please, can we see Rohit?", because by this time I had realised that Rohit was my strength. So once in a while, they would drop him in the morning and pick him up at night. I was tired of calling them up for my clothes, for Rohit and other things. I was also tired of their repeatedly cooked-up excuse, "Don't come home, everyone has infection in the house. If you come here, you will catch the infection and die." They frightened me. I stayed in the bungalow, not knowing what was going to happen.

Anyway, it was a nice place to be in. I had lovely neighbours. One was Mary and the other was Audrey. Mary was in her seventies. Audrey had a son called Paul. Both were very helpful. My mother did not know her surroundings and Mary showed her all the shops and shortcuts through the streets. She meant a lot to us. Every little bit from anyone meant so much to me. The expected help from my in-laws never arrived. The people who helped me will always be special to me and I will always be grateful to them. The only time I walked in this area and the road outside the bungalow was to accompany Mum to the shops one day.

Everything outside was covered in snow, brown slush covered the roads, people carefully treaded with the fear of falling. My shoes had no grip. I held my mother's hand and tried to bear my own weight to walk slowly through the slush-covered roads. My whole body was fragile and a little push would have unbalanced me. I could hardly breathe, my coat hung heavy on my aching shoulders. After the biopsy on the right side of my neck the blood did not flow properly to my right shoulder. It was always in a great deal of pain as if it was going to detach and fall on the floor. We decided to take a shortcut to the shops that Mary had told us about. The streets were unfamiliar just like this phase of my life, not knowing where I was going. We continued walking silently, trying to find the right way. I was very tired but somehow knew that Mum was not going to manage on her own, to buy everything I needed. Soon we found the signs for the shops across the road. I kept on touching my wig to make sure that it was on properly. The fear of it flying in the cold winds kept me alert.

We bought food, medicine and things that Rohit would need. My mother took me to a wool shop; she needed to do her knitting to pass her time while she was looking after me. We had talked enough of our circumstances and had realised that there were no answers to our problems, so it was hard for her to sit and do nothing. Mum asked me to choose a colour that I would like to wear. I chose a beautiful turquoise and white wool with a hint of silver in it. Mum bought all that she needed from different shops. Some of the shopkeepers wondered how I was doing, although I had never met them in my life. They mentioned Mary worrying about me having cancer. I was too tired, so we came back home in a taxi. I watched Mum start on my jumper and kept watching until it was completed. She never put it down until it was made. We were both aware that time may run out for me. I adored the jumper and wore it all the time.

That was a really hard winter. My thoughts were as frozen as the weather outside. I was broken in many places, and also the strongest in these broken places. Anyhow, I was glad of the jumper as it kept me warm.

December came and with it Ballu's twenty-first birthday. His in-laws insisted that he should celebrate his first birthday after his wedding. At first he did not want to, but then he suggested that everyone join us on his birthday in Liverpool so that he could be with me in the bungalow. My mother rang my in-laws, asking them and Sajan to join us and asked if they could please bring a saree for me for that day, or some sort of outfit as I did not have any decent clothes that fit me. They kept on promising till the last minute but as usual, I did not get any clothes. I had a yellow Indian suit, so tight on me that it was torn and stitched in places. My family kept waiting till the last minute for my clothes and none thought of buying any more, knowing my wardrobes were full and my current figure was temporary. So I wore what I had, to attend my brother's birthday.

I was so frail that I could not sit up, but felt happy to be alive and to spend time with Ballu. I sang after so many years. It reminded me of my childhood, and the times I spent with my friends, singing in every spare moment we had. It also reminded me of my music collection, lying in Sajan's house, which he was too cruel to consider bringing back to me. My sadness matched perfectly with some of the ghazals I sang. No one could feel what I felt, or see the true colours of my feelings.

By Christmas 1987, I had taken the eleventh treatment of chemotherapy. I spent that day in the hospital. All the patients in the ward received lovely gifts, not knowing whether they would be around for the following Christmas. I got soap, chocolate and a handkerchief. It was so lovely to receive those gifts from the hospital. I felt better being there, rather than anywhere else. At least I was cared for and loved there, with the unconditional positive regard that the staff gave me. I kept wondering all night if this was to be my last Christmas.

By the time I was to leave Liverpool after my twelfth chemotherapy appointment, I hated hospitals. I could not stand the echo of my reluctant feet through the long empty corridors. I hated that smell, the smell that made my stomach retch at just being in its presence. I hated those drips, hanging upside down on stands in every room. I hated the bare boards, gleaming with newly applied polish. I hated the dust-free windowsills, all of which were graced with identical flowers, in every room. I simply hated entering those doors that awaited my arrival, the same old voices whenever I passed them, saying, "Look who's here." I knew the nurses and patients weren't really surprised to see me, it was just a game they played. My silences were embarrassing to Mum at times. She usually covered for me, by telling people I wasn't well. The truth is, I was silent out of fear, not due to illness. I felt that breaking that silence would break my very essence, into pieces.

The following day, I expressed my urge to see Rohit. Mum did not know how to bring Rohit to me in a cold and dark night. I could not bear the thought of not seeing Rohit. I opened the front door, looked at the snow and found myself walking towards Audrey's house to see if her son Paul would help me. I felt that time was slipping through my hands faster than ever. I asked Audrey if Paul could take me to meet my son. It was eight o'clock at night. I wore the only nightdress I had and waited in the cold while Paul took his car out of the garage and took me to my in-laws' house. When I rang the bell, Kusha opened the door. She was holding Rohit. He had just taken a bath. He looked so adorable, I still remember. She was shocked to see me. I went in and held Rohit, quietly taking him upstairs to my room to get his nappies and a few clothes that my mother had knitted for him to pass time in the bungalow. I packed them in a bag and came down saying, "I'm taking Rohit with me." I do not think she had any answer ready for that, but checked my bag and said that I could not take the bag. I thanked and blessed Paul for the Christmas gift – the ride in his car to fetch my son.

I brought Rohit back with me. We did not have any nappies for the night. We had to do with the tea towels throughout the night. It was so cold that we had extra heaters on. Anyway, I was delighted to have him lying next to me. He spent the whole night, gasping for air and choking. My mother and I couldn't understand why he was doing this, and in the morning, Mum called Vita, to inquire. She was told that when Rohit would cry at home, Kadam would shout violently at him, especially when Rohit woke him up in the middle of the night. She said that Rohit was gasping because he was so afraid of being shouted at by Kadam.

The next day, my mother got baby food, clothes and other necessities for Rohit with the help of Anwar, the photographer at my wedding. If anyone asked me who helped me other than my family, I would say Anwar and his wife did. The whole family, including my nephews, came to be with me for Christmas and they all got beautiful toys for Rohit and clothes for me.

In the meantime, to guide me through the British system and to advise me on benefits available, the hospital sent a social worker to see what I was entitled to. The information and advice was a relief for some of my financial worries for the future. On the 31st of December 1987, I had my last chemotherapy treatment. By this time, I was vomiting blood as my stomach was bleeding after the chemotherapy, but now that Rohit was with me, I had no fear. Surprisingly, neither my in-laws nor Sajan ever rang for Rohit or came to pick him up. They never brought any of his clothes, they never rang to ask how he was doing and they didn't seem to bother. I guessed they had washed their hands of us then.

With the chemotherapy treatments over, in January 1988, I was taken to the hospital to undergo a final CAT scan to make sure that I was clear of cancer. Mum, Manu and I sat anxiously, pulses beating violently, awaiting the verdict.

I remember to this day, the sigh of relief that graced my mother's face when she heard the news. It was all clear, no more treatment, no more scans. I could go home. The only question remaining in my mind, as I looked over those faces, was which home I would go to. I looked at Manu holding Rohit tightly. I just followed him in silence, little knowing to which path my fate would guide me. But destiny rules and we obey.

21

Back in Newcastle

We came to the bungalow. Sanju and Chandni had packed everything, as if they had expected the verdict we received. The only thing that I needed, the only thing that was missing, was my diary, the only account of those three months, the ones that were supposed to be my last. Something possessed me, what it was is still a mystery, but I couldn't let go of Rohit, I wouldn't. I repeated to myself, that no matter what they kept, I had all I needed in my arms. That journey was the quietest of my life. Breaking the silence that had crept over us was simply unfitting to the aura.

By this time Sawi knew I had been very ill with cancer. She was furious with Dinki for not telling her earlier. I received lovely letters from Sawi with her wishes to see me before her departure for Canada. I regularly received loving mails from Dinki, Sawi and my nieces.

After arriving in Newcastle, my family never once gave me the slightest hint of my being a burden on them. They loved me, they wanted me to live for them, for Rohit and myself. I somehow wanted to live for Rohit but I felt I would be a burden on Manu the minute I left Liverpool. I did not want that. I got in touch with the social services and found out about my benefits, which helped. Although I was relieved to find help, it felt heavy to have to be dependent on social security. But I did not want to be in a position where

I needed to request financial help from my brothers, who were already doing so much for me.

Manu's house had three bedrooms, and there were five adults and three children living in it, including Rohit and I. I chose the lounge to be my room. Rohit and I would sleep in the lounge together. I used to make a bed on the lounge floor every night and we used to jump around and play as much as we wanted to and it was just wonderful. I used to watch the television every night, colour in my nephew's colouring books and write how I felt.

By this time, everyone knew I had been treated for cancer. During the day I would wear the second wig that Doctor Tappin had provided for me or the scarves that my mother had knitted for me during my time of illness. The first wig had been burnt when I left it hanging over a light bulb which someone had switched on; I suppose it was a source of ridicule for some, though only a person who hides behind that mask, knows its value.

I could only get in touch with my true self at night, when the whole house was asleep and I could take my wig off and feel my bald head and the thoughts inside it. Somehow life had changed. I knew deep down that my marriage was over, I was thrown back to my brother. People gave me sympathy which I did not need. They appreciated Manu's help during my illness and looked at Rohit and myself with a question mark.

My life ahead was really a question followed by a lot of other questions for which I had no answers. The whole environment was, in a way, new to me. Although I knew Chandni and Sanju, my nephews and brothers, somehow they were looking for the same old me that they knew before I was married. They could not see the mountains of problems I had to scale and the maze of difficulties I had to overcome to reach my present state. I had left behind my tradition, my culture and society.

It was hard to live amongst my family and not show my true feelings. Ballu had recently married, and Manu had his wife and children, and both of them had to carry on their normal lives, as I would have expected. The only thing that helped to keep me going was the children around me. My son was growing up and now talking a little bit. He once asked me why we slept in the lounge, and not in the bedroom. I explained that the floor was the best place to sleep on because there is no fear of falling off it, and even today, he loves sleeping on the floor in our lounge. We usually camp out in the lounge for a week over Christmas, watching movies and playing cards.

My family was relieved to have me here in Newcastle, relieved that my treatment was over and that they would not have to keep going back to Liverpool every week. Manu still took me to Liverpool once a month for check-ups with Doctor Tappin. All the staff in the ward loved to see me recovering. I enjoyed the rides with Manu, but whenever we drove in and out of Liverpool I felt very emotional. There had never been a time when I went to Liverpool and it had not rained. It must have been God's way of saying something to me. I felt that the sky cried with me. My mother went back to India with my Father in February 1988 as Dad had to see to his commitments in India, including Sawi.

By April, four months had passed since my treatment had finished. Sometimes in my mind, I kept hoping that Sajan would not want us to be with Manu any longer, knowing that I was recovering and my hair was coming back. I hoped for us to be together for our son. Aunt Nirmal suggested that I should ring Sajan. I phoned the shop a few times to hear Kadam tell me off for ringing. I only wanted to know where I stood in life. I rang again to speak to Sajan but Kadam would not let me speak to him. I asked him to give a message to Sajan, "Where do Rohit and I stand in his life?" He replied, "Do not ring us again, we are very busy and we will let you know soon."

22
Happiness, a Mirage

I was fully convinced that the tide of fortune would now flow in my favour. But again, it turned out to be only a change of mode of misfortunes, which, alongside social pressures, had robbed me since my marriage. I was taken by my family to Newcastle so that I might fully recoup and restore myself to robust health, but my family and society fully expected me to go back to Liverpool to Sajan, and fight for my rights.

In April 1988, Manu told me that we had to go to Bradford to see Sanju's mother, who was on dialysis. I readily agreed. However, I sensed something was not right. Sanju had brought a beautiful outfit for me, and helped me to get dressed, but when I sat in the car she wished me good luck. When I asked her why, she said, "Oh well, it has been a long time since you have been out of the house." I wanted to believe her. It felt good as we drove away.

On the journey, Manu tried to open me up by asking me about my views on my own experiences. He wondered if I would be prepared to divorce Sajan after all he had done to me, or try to begin a new life with him. He reminded me that Sajan had not cared for me and that I had my whole life in front of me. He basically asked me what I intended to do.

I replied, "Well, we will write him a letter and tell him that his baby needs him just as much as he needs his own parents. If he still needs his parents at twenty-six, Rohit needs both of his parents now So let's just see what he has to say to that."

I added, "It doesn't matter whether he keeps me or he remarries but I would hate it if he did not care for Rohit. It was not Rohit's fault that things did not turn out right for us, that I had cancer and that my in-laws did not want me. After all Rohit is also his baby and we should both love him. Rohit should not be deprived of love from his dad."

Manu took me to a solicitor in Bradford. He said "Well, this is to do with your intention of writing. I have brought you to this solicitor to give you some advice." He seemed to be the best for problems that the Indian community faced.

Manu told the solicitor about me. And after he had heard everything about my marriage, and how I was treated by Sajan and my in-laws, before and during my illness, he asked if I would consider divorcing Sajan. All of a sudden, Manu took some papers out of his pocket. They were divorce papers, addressed to me and signed by Sajan, in reply to my phone call to Kadam. I received an unbearable shock when Manu started discussing the divorce proceedings. I learnt that my husband wished to divorce me on the charge of unreasonable behaviour and unbecoming conduct on my part. In fact, the shoe was on the other foot, it was my in-laws who had shown unbecoming conduct and unreasonable behaviour towards a helpless, innocent woman. I just could not believe it. I sobbed. It was too soon for me to fight another battle.

The solicitor said it did not mean that I had to go through with it. We could fight the case and defend it to prove that I was not unreasonable. He said that it was all mere accusations and we would prove him wrong, and all the rest.

We came back, and from that night, I did not sleep at all. It was a new turn in the course of events. I had received divorce papers. I got married at the age of twenty-one, had a baby at twenty-two, had cancer at twenty-three and received divorce papers before the age of twenty-four. There was no way I would remarry for any reason. I just felt funny, at the irony of fate. Things around me were moving fast.

My brothers were getting busier in their business. Although they did not have much time, they cared, loved and provided me with all that I needed.

Everyone moved on with their lives but time stood still for me. It was a rather hard time. We received letters from the court. Going to the courts and solicitors became a tortuous task, it became a routine. My heart sank at the thought of being divorced. In a way, I thought it was better to get divorced than to hang around or go back and be tortured again. After all, they did not want me. But then I was frightened: would they take the baby away from me, would Sajan want the custody and how would he see Rohit? Even if I divorced him, would he come to see the baby and how would I feel? All these questions, and there was no one I could talk to. I used to write whatever I could, as little as possible, so no one would pick it up and read it.

Lots of people from Liverpool and Newcastle became involved, mainly for gossiping. About twenty of my relatives went to Liverpool to talk with Kadam about my future. Some of their friends had come from Liverpool to attend this meeting. Everyone kept saying, "Everything is going to be all right, you'll first get better and be back here in Liverpool, with your husband."

I knew deep down that nobody wanted me in that house. All these talks, discussions and all these people, their words meant nothing. They all had attended my wedding and blessed me but their blessing did not last very long. Here, the whole society was interested in the story of my life. I wondered about Chandni and Sanju, how they would feel if I was divorced and stayed on with them for the rest of my life. I wondered how they would treat me, as I had experienced how so many people had changed in the past under various circumstances. I tried to be brave, but meeting people and carrying on with life was getting harder. I became a recluse. After Mum found out about the divorce papers, she flew back to England, leaving Dad in India to handle his affairs.

Although I was really low, constantly having to stand up for myself had shattered me deep down. I told everyone to leave me alone and had a hysterical attack and kept repeating to myself that I did not want to be back in Liverpool. Suffering can cause fragmentation, isolation and meaninglessness. In the fit of this depression some negative emotions took over me and I took an overdose of painkillers, the name escapes me, and almost instantly confessed that I had taken them. Mum slapped me as hard as she could, and rang for an ambulance. No one else uttered a word. Manu watched my breakdown in bewilderment, thinking that his own struggle was in vain, the struggle he took upon himself to give me another chance in life. I was in the hospital for three days, followed by an array of counselling sessions.

My family was anxious and worried, not only for me but for Sawi as well.

23

Ms Davison – My Angel

After the treatment of cancer and the subsequent divorce, I was once again left alone, along with my child, in this vast world. In British law, if a couple lives separately for more than two years, divorce procedures can occur without any other grounds. Such was my case. I decided to fight the allegations against me, and in court, my in-laws could not prove that I was an unreasonable person. The judge however, stated that because of the said law, it did not matter who was guilty of what. I was saddened that in these proceedings, I could not recover any of my belongings, as my in-laws had kept my valuables with their relatives, denying their existence. It was not so much the vast monetary value of these objects that hurt me, it was more the sentimental value that I had attached to them.

I was still living with Manu and Ballu, but felt as if I was an unsaid burden on them. After all, every human being has his or her own responsibility and commitments. The nearest of one's kith and kin cannot be at one's beck and call for the whole of one's life. They also have a life of their own to lead. Moreover, any self-respecting person doesn't want to live a parasite's life, dependent on another.

It dawned upon me that I should stand on my feet and try to lead such a life that may not be construed as a burden even on my closest relations. Rohit was only eighteen months old when I had to move about for organising my life and visiting clinics and hospitals for medical check-ups and various other tests. It was inconvenient to always take Rohit with me, so I thought of fixing him up in a crèche for a few hours daily. It was with the intention of finding out about such a crèche that I knocked at No. 5 Grasmere Place. After listening to my requirements, the lady, Ms Davison Carrick, offered to look after Rohit whenever I was to go for a medical check-up or attend any urgent engagement. Meeting Ms Davison was a providential blessing. She was an angel in my life, a motherly figure with a caring, kind and generous personality whose philanthropic spirit beamed through her smile. She was soft-spoken, loved her family, loved shopping, and hated flying to the extent that to date, she does not have a passport.

I had to move on. I thought of learning to drive and looked around for an instructor and started to take driving lessons. Whenever my instructor came to give me a lesson, there was Ms Davison to take care of Rohit. From then on, she was keen to see Rohit and each time I needed her help, she was there for us. When Rohit was two years old, Ms Davison came for his birthday.

I enjoyed Rohit's second birthday more than the first. Rohit received a beautiful gold chain from Manu. This was the first piece of jewellery we owned after I had been ill and had lost all of my belongings to my in-laws. I had lost everything, material or otherwise, to them. They were cruel to keep Rohit's clothes, toys and other things. I can never forget that, ever. Although things can be bought and thrown away, the feelings attached to Rohit's belongings were too precious for me. My heart will always long for them.

I got my medical file transferred from Liverpool to Newcastle because obviously it was more convenient. This saved me having to drive through the memory lanes of Liverpool every time I needed a check-up. Although I seemed to be moving around in my family circle, my life remained fixed with ill health and side effects of the treatment, looking after Rohit and not knowing my future. I felt everyone needed space from each other, as it was so crowded at times with all of us living in one house.

By this time I was reading psychological books to help me pull through and not wait for anyone to give me a hand. I also strongly felt that Sajan leaving me did not mean that I was going to be dead. I had to pick myself up and pull myself together before anyone else tried to give me a hand, because I would not want that. I felt strong enough. Reading all those books on cancer treatment helped me realise what I had. I got over all the treatment and I was recovering. It was time I stood up for my son and myself.

At the same time, I thought, "Wait a minute, where am I going to be when my brothers separate and live their own lives?" I had to become independent and give them their space.

Anyhow, having Ms Davison was like having a second parent for Rohit. All I wanted to do now was to travel to India to reassure my parents, meet my sisters and nieces and share Rohit with them.

24

1989 – India

In June 1989, I flew with my experiences to India and took Rohit with me. Billa, who had been to see me in England, accompanied me to be with my sisters. Rohit's *mundan* meant a lot to all of us. I had dreams of having a grand party in my hometown to celebrate this ceremony. I was in high spirits and had great expectations of having a good time after all I had suffered. I had a list of guests and I knew exactly how wonderful this day would be for all of us.

India was too hot for both of us, Rohit and me, as we were used to the British climate. I was warmly welcomed by Dinki and my nieces, and because of the excessive heat, they took both of us to Dehra Dun, where it's considerably cooler than Punjab. They were so happy to see me alive and to see Rohit for the first time. I had to take care of Rohit as he had diarrhoea in the first ten days, so we could not travel to Punjab, where Sawi was. I wanted to be there as soon as possible. I spoke to her over the telephone, and could feel the eagerness between us to see each other, as it had been three years since we had last met.

Sawi wrote to me saying that she was dying to see us. Dinki, her family, Rohit and I reached Ludhiana, Punjab on the 2nd of July 1989 to stay at my parents' house. Mum and Dad were away to Haridwar, by the Ganges. They usually spent their summer months in our home in Rishikesh, but I was thrilled to be in our home in Ludhiana. We rang Sawi to let her know that we would visit her on Wednesday. In the meantime, Sawi's husband had arrived back from Canada after a few years. We could not travel to the airport to receive him due to Rohit, my health and the heat. Sawi was planning to attend Rohit's function and fly to Canada with her husband to settle there with her two daughters.

On Wednesday morning I woke up as the phone rang. Dinki and her family were still in bed. I answered the phone and a stranger said that he was a well-wisher and had rung up to inform me that my sister Sawi had been murdered and her dead body was lying at the morgue. He told me that if we wanted to see the body, we had to be there quickly, before it was cremated. It just blew my head and I shouted. I could not resist being furious and told him off for saying things like that to me over the phone. I could not believe what he was saying, for I had spoken to her a couple of days earlier. Billa took the phone from me as he heard me shouting.

Within minutes, we were on the move. I was absolutely devastated, shocked and stunned. It was another blow, as if I had not had enough. Dinki fainted when she heard about Sawi. Everyone rushed out to get help and to inform others in the community. I was the only one left with the children. I phoned the police in the village where she lived, to make sure they kept the body till we got there. Her in-laws had not informed us. I approached one of the tenants, Ashok, in my dad's property and requested him to accompany me to the morgue. Although it was no more than twenty-five to thirty miles away, it seemed like a long way and it took ages to get there. I had been standing upright all morning, strong but exhausted, knowing exactly where I was going. Some other tenants travelled along to take me to my destination, but I only knew one of them, Ashok. I could see the sun shining, its rays heating all around me, yet feeling cold within as I rode along the Nawanshahr broken roads, lined with dust, from Ludhiana to Nawanshahr, where I would find my sister. Time was not fast enough to match my fearful heartbeat and my racing thoughts and the journey seemed never-ending. I looked only to reaching my destination, forgetting myself, forgetting who I was. I was torn between my love and responsibility towards Sawi, and my medical condition.

I saw none of the people from Sawi's family whom I had expected to be there, only a few well-fed, bribed policemen. I smelt dust, tears and death around me as I approached these men, sitting leisurely, watching me as if I were an entertainment programme.

Suddenly I became like a rock. I went forward, demanding to see the body of my sister. They smiled, saying that they needed to see my identification, and that the body needed to be cremated. I stood firmly in front of them. Some voices from the tenants lingered in the air, "Let her see her sister's body," as if they knew my pain.

After tearing my gut, shouting and begging before them, I was finally taken to a cramped, dusty room. They opened the lock and stood back, leaving me alone to lift the iron shutter. I did so swiftly, showing that I had no fear of them. I searched the room through my tears, and saw a trolley. Her body lay there, quietly waiting for me. Our reunion was one-sided. Impulsively I shouted her name, my hands fumbling, grasping her wrists, checking her. I lifted the sheet, my eyes raking over her form as I refused to believe what was before me. She was mine, but couldn't say a word to me. Silence. I stopped crying, looking about me only with anger as I demanded to see the superior officers. The universe stood still from that moment. I had changed from a homely girl to a responsible woman, capable of bearing the liability of my sibling, who would want me to keep her body for the family. I lowered my eyes, walking out in disbelief, hearing the shutter slam down behind me as I went to the telephone.

I called the superintendent of the police department. He came within minutes. He was educated, polite and understanding, which under the circumstances was unexpected. I explained to him that my family was away, and I had come from England, and that they couldn't be here till the next day. I requested him not to cremate her in my family's absence. The older shopkeepers, silent up to that point, started arguing. "She's dead now, it's too hot, the body will start to smell, she should be cremated … there's nothing left of her to take home."

I moved to the shutter, sitting outside, my eyes flickering over them, challenging them, knowing that to reach her they would have to pass me. I sat alone, feeling my thoughts sink in, knowing that the love I had felt, that I had kept for her, the gifts I had brought with me, the promises of good times, had all turned to tears and ashes before me. I knew I would never be the same; I had lost a part of me, a part of my identity from that day. At this moment I looked alone, but I felt her presence there with me.

I met a few policemen and went straight to the hospital from the morgue, to find the doctor who had dealt with her. He tried telling me that my sister had taken too many pain killers by mistake and had died. As soon as he realised that I knew a bit about medicines myself, he changed the story. All I wanted to know was how she had died, to learn the cause of her death. The officials around me harassed me further by taking their time in asking me to complete the formalities. I rang Manu in England to inform him. He came to India within twelve hours.

In the meantime, Billa brought the court order for the post-mortem to be done. The result showed us that she was poisoned.

Sawi was no more. The terror, shock and sadness was so deep and so hurtful that none of us knew what to do with it. My mum and dad came. My mother could not believe it. Sawi's body was brought home. Manu and my father carried out the rituals at her funeral. Nobody could look each other in the eye because of what we had all seen. By now, my dad was having serious psychological problems with manic depression. The one who wears the shoe knows where the shoe pinches. My father, the head of the household, was watching his beloved family crumble around him.

Mum is still in shock and even today looks for Sawi, who had a scar on her forehead, who was so special. She was the best girl Mum had. She was God-fearing, down to-earth and simple. The entire time I stayed in India, I ran around, watching my family go in and out of the courts to fight for justice. We found out from the neighbourhood that her in-laws and husband had beaten her up the night before. It was rumoured that her husband had another wife in Canada. It was believed that they all conspired in her death. Indian law courts take ages to provide justice, and the case is still in the trial court.

With Sawi's picture held close to my chest and with heavy hearts, Dinki, Billa and my nieces took Rohit and me to the Ganges, where we performed his *mundan* very quietly, sitting on the bank of the river. Our minds were not there that day, but I had no choice but to have the ceremony at that time Because it had to be done before Rohit was three. I placed Sawi's photo beside me and cried all through the ceremony, looking at the flowing, shimmering water of the Ganges, where we had immersed her ashes. I had brought small gifts for everyone and when I looked at Sawi's share of them, it broke my heart. From then on Rohit called Dinki, Badi Mamma.

My whole family ran around to sort out this murder case. My father was so ill that he did not know what was going on. Everyone did his best. All the suffering I had faced on account of my illness, the divorce, being a single parent or being a burden on the family seemed so little in front of Sawi's death. She had left her daughters behind, Anu and Vanu, aged five and four respectively. I wanted to take them away with me. But I never saw them, as Sawi's in-laws' family ran away to hide from the police. Her husband had washed his hands of any obligation to Sawi, and the rituals he should have undertaken after her death were performed by Dad and Manu. I made Rohit touch her dead body just before it was cremated, as Sawi so much wanted to be touched by Rohit.

I came back from India heartbroken, and brought back many unspoken feelings for Sawi. It seemed so unfair. Life had changed for all of us. Manu moved into a new house. He called his house 'Sawi' to keep her alive amongst us. Billa and my mum ran in and out of the courts in India to seek justice for Sawi. My Dad became extremely ill with the psychological shock of Sawi's death. Manu and Ballu called up from England daily to find out the progress of Sawi's case.

Under no circumstances did I want to be seen as a problem to my family, but Manu insisted I stay with him. However, I still looked for somewhere to live independently. While I lived with Manu in his new house, I remember a day when a distant relative of mine, an aunt, came to see Manu and his new house. My aunt was shown around the home, including my bedroom. She looked down on me and said, "Oh, what more does a person like you want after having this room." Then she paused but could not somehow justify my having that room. The tone of her voice gave me the feeling that she was saying that I did not deserve it. Although I did not like her attitude, I felt sorry for her shallow judgement. She left me with a great awareness of how society perceived me. I thanked her in my heart for behaving the way she did.

I had great difficulty in sleeping. Every time I closed my eyes I could see Sawi's face, as if she wanted to talk to me. I was not frightened of her as I knew she would never harm me. I stayed awake to hear what she had to say to me. One day my aunt Aruna told me to get my eyes checked as they looked tired and strained, as if I had not slept for months. My GP suggested I see a counsellor.

The counsellor was very experienced; he counted my losses from 1983 to 1989: losing touch with my country, my home, my parents, my friends and my culture. I had lost my married life, status, health, social respect, my home and my money and on top of that, the greatest loss of all, my sister. I had no sense of direction or recognition in life. My counsellor taught me to live with the fact that in my heart Sawi would always be alive. I had so much to tell Sawi, but I could not. After a few sessions Sawi became part of my life. I was taught how to talk to her in my mind, tell her anything that I wanted to, and I did just that. It helped me to sleep better. My counsellor also used cushions, large and small, scattered in a room, leaving no place to walk around them, as a metaphor for my mental state. I had to learn to place them in an orderly pile, from the largest to the smallest, so as to clear the room for some light and thereby clear the clutter in my mind.

I desperately needed some peace of mind, but from my past experiences, I doubted that I would get any. My parents knew my wish to live independently and agreed whole-heartedly. Although Dad was ill, he told me never to remarry and love Rohit with all my heart for as long as I lived.

Manu was now busy taking Dad in and out of hospital for treatment for acute depression, diabetes and arthritis. Dad stopped drinking totally, and it seemed like a miracle to all of us. But it was sad to see him suffer from poor health.

25
My Home

It was 1990 when I finally found a place for Rohit and myself because I knew everyone had to move on in life and I could not be left behind. I knew that if I did not move then, I never would. My new house was one door away from Ballu and Chandni's house and that was very convenient for us. It was socially acceptable for a young divorced Indian woman with a small child to live near her family and not be completely alone. I knew living close to my family would mean more security and we could easily help each other.

From March 1990 I had to learn to live with Rohit in my own home. Although we were close to our family, parting from them was difficult. But we needed space for ourselves. It was my choice. I was never taught to lead a life like this, but I loved my house, it was beautiful. I thanked God and my brothers in my heart for making this possible. For the first fifteen days, Ms Davison stayed with us, to help us adjust. She explained that my brother was just a few walls away, and always there if I needed him. After a long time, I wrote my name and address in a diary. I lived at Number Seven, with my brother at Number Nine. It felt so good that we would never be homeless again. It was God's way of chastising my ex-husband, firstly for thinking that I would die from cancer and secondly for making us homeless. My God had been carrying me throughout my troubles. I felt special and closer to God. Still, I was afraid and alone at night in my house, but I could not tell anybody because not everybody had liked the idea of my having my own home in the first place.

I did everything just for Rohit. After remembering the harsh words of my aunt, her despicable way of looking down on me and my bedroom in Manu's house, which had hurt me so much, I did not want anyone else to say anything like that to my son. To give Rohit the space he needed to grow, I had to move ahead with his needs in mind. It gave me so much pride that the fear of being alone weighed a lot less than the joy of being proud, coping and taking on the responsibility of my son and myself. I hardly saw any of my extended family who lived in the town. None of them came to our house to see how I was doing. I often saw them at social gatherings or at the temple. My brothers with their families always visited us on weekends. My parents were very happy to see me alive and taking care of Rohit. They always blessed us from the depths of their hearts.

Manu used to say, "When you were living with me I would see you every day but now it is difficult because you have moved out to be on your own." After a while, he understood that I needed to carry on and he was happy for me. My son and I needed our independence and identity.

This year yielded another happy occasion in the family. Ballu and Chandni had their first child in December 1990, a baby girl, whom they named Jaya. I wasn't well enough to accompany Chandni to the hospital, but I was amazed at how small and beautiful the baby was, and seeing Ballu as a father was a very happy occasion for me.

The fear of cancer, the prying eyes of society and my own responsibility and commitment required a lot of strength. Everyone wanted to see how long I would cope.

26
Sublimation through Suffering

After Sawi's death, it was unbearable for Dinki to be alone in India. Dinki and her daughters came over to England permanently. The whole family grew extremely busy in seeing to her. I was very pleased to have her nearby. I had so many desires to fulfil with her, but somehow I could not connect with her, as we were two different personalities. I had led a completely different life when compared to hers. Although we met every day, we never touched each other on a heart-to-heart level. She was missing Sawi. Realising that I only had one sister left, after Sawi, I tried my best to love, care and make her comfortable with all my ability at the time. Looking back now, I can see that she could never have imagined the strength and effort I had to put in to give her all that I did. While I wanted support from her, she was expecting it from me. I started feeling tired and ill with a lot of pain all over my body. I was diagnosed with rheumatoid arthritis. I cried a lot and told Manu about the diagnosis.

He took me for a walk in his garden, held my hand and said, "Aren't you lucky, at least you are alive to have this pain, what if you had died in 1987, you would not have this pain in 1990, would you?"

That made me smile, he was right. I thought, after all I was alive and when you are alive, you can do a lot of things, and learn a lot of things. There are all sorts of treatments and cures for a person who is alive. I thought of Sawi who was no more and whom we could never bring back, and felt grateful for having life. Yet I felt isolated in my own pain, in my own world. I felt as if I was far away from my own home, my family and society.

I had to attend appointments and I did not want to burden anyone further. I still had to go to GPs for regular check-ups and medication. Life had to move on. Ms Davison accompanied me everywhere I needed to be, often driving me there herself, as I had no other means of getting anywhere.

On one of my visits to the Newcastle General Hospital, I met a nurse who found me to be very depressed and suggested I should join a cancer group. I was given a leaflet and a number where I could contact Vera Bateman. She belonged to the Hexham Cancer Group in Northumberland. She immediately came to see me and to comfort me. She took me with her to meet the other members in her group. They were all cancer sufferers, and understood the pain that I had suffered during my illness. They could not, however, see the other pains that were deeply rooted inside me.

The cancer group helped me a lot. Their support, love and healing treatments were so powerful, they started to bring me out of the state I was in. They gave me light, gave me the necessary support, and the people running that group were marvellous. They helped everyone in that group because most of the members had known cancer. The group was like a world on its own, an escape from the outside world. I had never experienced so much love amongst people. We all needed it and we all shared it. It was so soothing to be there. The time spent there was the best time I had throughout the week. I attended the group every Tuesday night, with Rohit, for four years; some people I knew had recurrence of cancer and died, and I would get upset for weeks remembering them. At such times, I stopped my regular visits, as I was afraid of becoming emotionally attached to people and then losing them.

God certainly wanted me to let go of things and move on. After passing through such vicissitudes in life, I had pertinent and rich experiences which a normal person even at the ripe old age of eighty fails to have. Gold gets purified after passing through fire, dross is blown away and the yellow metal in its purest form remains in the crucible. Similarly, after passing through the flames of life, though physically enfeebled, I had spiritually become very strong. I had gained a higher and greater understanding of life. The greater the number of battles and wars a soldier engages himself in, the more experienced and seasoned he turns out to be. In my life also, I braved one battle after the other. My vision of life had soared to a very high plane. Petty things and incidents had become very trivial and insignificant for me, especially when compared to my own illness, and Sawi's tragic passing. I developed in my personality a stupendous confidence. I started the next chapter of my life with a new purpose. I tried to channel and sublimate my energies. In 1991, I passed my driving test. My educational career which I had abandoned in 1983 was recommenced in 1993, by studying counselling at Newcastle University. There developed in me a strong urge to do something to alleviate the sufferings of the less fortunate. In September of that same year, I became an aunt to Ballu's second daughter, Geetika. Having remembered not being there at Jaya's birth, I wanted to be with Chandni through her labour, and Ballu and I accompanied her into the labour room. In a sense, I was fearful for Ballu, as this was his second daughter, and I knew how our society regarded the birth of a second daughter in a household. Nevertheless, I loved Geetika, keeping her for the first forty days of her life, with Chandni and Jaya, in my home.

Being an Asian woman, going through all the experiences of my life, I was still very much restricted by my own values as an Indian. Even the killer disease did not free me from the shackles of culture. If it had been Sajan having cancer, everyone would openly have asked me to look after him, and do things in the best possible way to help him through the disease. However, no one really cared, no one looked at it that way for me. Even today in our society women do not have easy access to justice. I depended entirely on prayers.

When I think of it now, I understand culture and our society. Anything I do, wear or eat has a cultural meaning. Most of the time when I overeat, it brings back memories of being deprived of food by Sajan when I was ill. My mother fed me then but it felt so wrong. When I can afford food now, I buy, cook and eat and feed others and feel happy. When I dress up, it means a lot to me. I feel special, telling myself that I deserve it.

People cannot see through my emotions and I often catch them making certain remarks about me. I strongly feel that if it were them instead of me, they would not survive as I did. I often laugh at their triviality.

I had kept a diary during my illness. In 1988, I used to write in it every day for Rohit, in case I did not live long enough to tell him. On the last day when I left Liverpool, I looked all over the place, but I could not find it. I searched for it in my mind, again and again, trying to remember where it could have gone. I think somebody picked it up and kept it away deliberately to help me move forward in life. It was God's way of telling me to let it go.

It took me years to learn that it must be God's way of saying – "It's all over. Look up to the future, rather than the past." If I want to drive ahead I cannot and must not look into the rear view mirror. I do not want to think of my miserable past, but I will always remember the lessons learnt from it. I applied this thinking to the loss of my sister. I blamed myself, for the longest of times, for not going to see her myself, and for relying on Dinki and Billa to take me. My brothers were in England at the time, my father in Haridwar, and the only person who could have taken me was Billa. However, society would have raised eyebrows once more, as it would have been inappropriate for a divorced woman to travel alone with her brother-in-law, to her sister's home. Dinki, being protective, wanted me to rest, and stay out of the heat, and because she did so, with the best of intentions, I couldn't see Sawi before she died.

It makes me sick sometimes, the things we have to go through, the punishments we are given, through no fault of our own. In being an Indian woman who obeys our society's made-up standards, I have suffered this kind of treatment quite often. If I was to relive my past, I would not have put up with social rules or expectations and would have travelled alone to visit my sister Sawi.

My family and the experiences of life have made me look beyond the relationships I have with each one of the members in my family. My value system has changed. I see beyond the obvious, and realise that life is not something that should be wasted. I can understand those people who have gone through cancer, who have had to fight to live a bit longer. I bet they have the same value system as I do, feel the same feelings, and realise that not very many people understand. I now believe in living for the moment and doing all I can for myself and others, while I can.

Life becomes a gift and it is very precious after you have won the battle against cancer. Every minute of life is important because you are not sure whether you will have another day or not. You want to do so much, you want to do everything that comes to mind, because you are alive today. No matter how many years go past being in remission, you still have that fear of having cancer again. It is a constant reminder; anything you do in your life, any action you take, any step you take, you are grateful for it. Above all, it means a lot to meet people. You open your heart to those you love, and you start to love the world around you. You feel sensitive, especially for the ones who go through the same treatment, or a similar situation in life. You feel the hurt that ill people fell much more than those who take health for granted.

Necessities in life are collected for their practical value. Anything other than a necessity is merely an item that helps use up a little bit of the precious life that you possess. These items provide superficial pleasures, hiding a person's real self from the world. I have learned through my experiences that it does not matter how much material wealth a person possesses. I have learned to make friends from all walks of life who will accept me for who I am as a person. I have also learned to throw away items that do not reflect who I am, believing in the notion that simplicity in life is often the best policy. It has changed my overall outlook so much now that no material possessions hold value in my eyes. The people I love, and those that reciprocate that love unconditionally are all that matter to me in life.

27

Further Education

A longside my rheumatoid arthritis, I developed asthma, which greatly affected my breathing, and restricted where I could go, as I couldn't stand to be in a smoky environment. My health was degenerating further, and I was tired of keeping a brave face before my family. Physically and mentally, I was worn out, and I needed a release from the monotonous life I had been living since my return to Newcastle. I turned to reading, starting with a few books on diets that are beneficial to cancer patients. As I began to read more, I delved into more psychological books, and began to realise that I needed to learn more about my own thoughts, and their meaning. After reading a few inspirational works, it didn't take much to realise that I needed to become more independent of my family, and take positive steps to enhance my own standard of life, rather than taking backward steps, or not taking any steps at all.

A friend of mine, Fiona, lived only a few doors away from my own. Upon discussing my thoughts and recent revelations with her, she recommended that I attend Newcastle University with her, for a short adult learning course, titled 'Introduction to Counselling, Part One'. I saw this as an opportunity, firstly to get out of the house a little, with Fiona's support, and secondly, to meet people who were possibly in the same situation as I was, or at least, people who could understand my ideas. Finally, I felt that with this course, I would gain a greater insight into who I was, as a person.

The course was only running for twelve weeks. I would attend every Thursday night for two hours. The course thrilled me, and I began applying the knowledge I gained to myself, sitting back and analysing myself. Being in that stimulating atmosphere, with people who genuinely wanted to understand me, rather than understanding me out of obligation, was very comforting. I began to open up, bit by bit, revealing any thoughts that I may have repressed.

Fiona left the course after Part One. Her children and life, I feel, were too demanding for her to continue. But I couldn't bring myself to leave, and finding my own means of transport, I continued enthusiastically through Part Two, opening up further with each session. In one session, I coined the phrase, 'the more you know, the more you know you don't know', and this perfectly sums up how I felt, wanting to learn as much as I possibly could.

I feel that the most important thing I learned during this period, was that there is no shame in sharing one's inner fears and troubles in life, especially in an atmosphere that allows it, through support and kindness. Before this course, the only support I would receive would be along the lines of, 'pull yourself together', but after revealing my life to the people who were studying with me, I realised that my own experiences were unique, and in some cases, devastating. I realised that my life was far from ordinary.

After seeing my mental state somewhat uplifted, and after having less of the close proximity that we once had, my family began to think that I was well settled in my own home, and becoming more independent. I feel that in some ways, it was good that I was left to tend to my own troubles, and look after my child. It was a difficult adjustment however, being seen as a normal and functioning person from the outset, as I knew that I was not.

My education taught me not to expect anything from anyone. Whatever anyone did for me was their personal choice and a blessing to me. I tried to accept as little help as possible and maintain my brave face, especially socially. I did not want pity because I knew by now who was genuinely there for me, and who I could go to if I needed help in any aspect of life. I felt certain most people's show of concern towards me was more of a facade, an obligation. It was for the sake of tradition or culture or society, not really meant for me. I was growing up fast. I was understanding issues of my life easier than ever before.

As time passed, I regularly attended classes at the university. I was twenty-nine years old, nearing thirty. Lots of times, Manu tried to persuade me to get married again. But my dad never once felt the need for me to be remarried and somehow, I knew he understood me better than everyone else in the family. Manu used to say, "Life is too long, you need to have someone beside you. Children grow up and move out, and never look back. Who will you live for?"

But somehow I knew that I had taken the responsibility of bringing Rohit up, and I wanted to do it properly. Being pragmatic, I would not ruin his life by getting married again, or at least until the day I knew he was well settled. My past experience of marriage, my present situation and the sight of many unhappy married couples within society, made my determination to keep myself away from any such attachment even stronger. I felt I was better off bringing up Rohit alone and staying protected in the shadow of my family. My siblings were becoming well known for their achievements in business and my brothers considered me lucky for them. I felt touched by their good-heartedness.

Although the need to socialise was there, I could not really see myself attending a social circle that was outside my families, as I didn't feel that I fitted in anywhere else. I realised that whatever I said or did had a philosophical meaning, far more serious than others around me. I had forgotten to be lighthearted or to spend time without thinking deeply. I carried on as best as I could. My body hurt, no matter where I was or what I was doing.

Rohit was growing up fine. He was a good, disciplined and healthy child. In the past, he had attended a private nursery with the help of my family, as the other boys attended private schools and Manu wanted the same for Rohit. My wish was to see him able to carry on his studies, not by being funded by my family, but through merit and hard work. So I took him out of the nursery and sent him to an ordinary state school, nearer the house. I told him to work hard to prove that sending him to a private school would be a good idea. It was my dream to give him a good education and to see him achieve his potential.

Rohit wanted to attend the same school as Vaz, The Royal Grammar School, reputed for being one of the best private schools in the city. In 1995, when Rohit was eight years old, he passed the entrance exam for the RGS Junior school. My family, especially my parents, were thrilled for him, and I knew deep down that attending this institution would be greatly beneficial for his future.

As Rohit got more engrossed in his schooling, I found my days to be lacking purpose. There was little that I could feasibly do around the house, so I decided to continue my education further. I applied to Newcastle University for a course in counselling, which I would attend part time. It gave me great pleasure to see both of us leaving for school in the mornings, and gave meaning to my lonely hours, when Rohit wasn't around the house.

Education at this level was entirely different from the education I had received in India. I had to do assignments and project work, which I had never done before, and thus the intellectual adjustment was a very difficult one. I had never had a male tutor in India, as a tutor-student relationship is seen as a relatively intimate one in our society, which did not allow it at the time. I further realised the farcical nature of that society.

My tutor, Percival Gilbert Medd, known by everyone as Gil, was a true inspiration for me. I often feel that he attempted to tailor his words to apply to the situations I had faced in life, making them of most use to me. This attitude further fuelled my wish to study, and I worked very hard to attain the best grades that I could. Although Gil retired a few years after I left the university, we have kept in touch with each other through Christmas cards.

28

Black Ice

The side-effects of chemotherapy had created a plethora of ailments and infirmities in me. Because none of these troubles could be seen from the outside, I was often mistaken to be a fit and healthy person, and the expectations of others far outweighed what I was capable of. Adding to the pressure, Dinki began taking Manu's side, saying that I should remarry. She said that I had proved my point, raising Rohit alone up to this stage, but now it was time I settled down. I feel that deep down, Dinki and I are still very different people. I wanted to be independent, and able to run my own life proudly. I feel that Dinki was too shallow to understand that by this time, I had developed an innate psychological aversion to marriage and the notion of such a contract altogether. She saw me as a stigma, a bad example to her own children. Since they had an aunt who was divorced, and thus in her mind, disgraced in society, she felt it boded ill for their future marriages. Her attitude to life saddened me, but I understood why it was so. By now I knew our society's judgemental viewpoint towards a young divorced woman.

On Christmas Eve in 1992, I got a phone call from Ballu, who said teasingly that my father had come to England as a surprise for Christmas and was currently at his house. I joked with him, telling him that he was lying, and that Dad wouldn't have come without telling me. I put the phone down, and in a burst of happiness, ran out of my door to Ballu's house. I was so excited, that I forgot to change out of my slippers, and slipped suddenly on black ice on Ballu's driveway. I felt everything go blank, and quite possibly the sharpest pain I've ever felt coursed through my body. I screamed for help, and Fiona's husband, Paul, ran outside to help me. A few minutes later, Ballu was driving me to the hospital.

My head was spinning badly, and although he made a point of driving very slowly, I felt as though he was speeding. I was taken into the emergency room, and X-rayed almost immediately. I was given a strong dose of painkillers, and told that my back was badly bruised and swollen, and that I should be confined to bed rest.

After hearing this diagnosis, I thought that bruising wasn't so bad, and because of my burning wish to spend time with Dad over Christmas, I neglected the doctor's orders. Whenever I felt pain in my back, I would tell myself that it was probably my arthritis playing up, and continue with whatever I was doing. My father, and Mum's brother, Mani Uncle, both told me repeatedly that a back injury is a serious matter, and that I should slow down and take more care, but as I got more used to the pain, I carried on with day-to-day life, namely taking care of Rohit, and going to University.

After a few days, I started having severe cases of vertigo, and kept falling over, as if I had no coordination in my body whatsoever. I tried an assortment of therapies, including private physiotherapy, aromatherapy, hydrotherapy, acupuncture, manipulation and likon therapy, which were all temporary pain relievers over the following months. After all of these failed to give me any lasting physical benefit, I sought the help of Doctor Walker, who was my consultant rheumatologist at the Freeman Hospital.

Doctor Walker diagnosed me as having two prolapsed discs in my spine, and ankylosing spondylosis.

This condition is a chronic form of arthritis that affects the spinal joints, making them fuse together. Doctor Walker tried sending me to a pain clinic, thinking I may be exaggerating the pain that I was having. He referred me to a psychotherapist, and although this didn't help me physically, it helped me mentally to voice the pain I was having, and it also helped ease the depressed state I had fallen into because no one would believe how much pain I was in.

I would stay up all night, read, write or maybe do a bit of embroidery until I got really tired, but no matter what I did, I was never in a comfortable position to sleep. I took antidepressants occasionally and life seemed harder than ever. But what really hurt and annoyed me the most was that my family, as well as the doctors, thought that my pain was an excuse for me to cry when I could not get my way. Rohit was helping me as much as he could. It got harder for both of us. He was the only one who could understand me and was always there for me. Ms Davison helped me a lot with my hospital appointments and accompanied me most of the time.

In the half-term of my counselling course, I was idly chatting with Gil, saying that I would love to fly to India and have a break for a couple of weeks.

He looked at me and said, "Why don't you?"

"Just like that?" I asked, and he replied "Yes, just like that. Why don't you?"

I came home, talked to Rohit and told him that I would love to go for a break, and he said, "OK, Mum, you do just that."

I made arrangements to leave Rohit with Chandni, and told the family that I was taking the first available flight out. No one protested much, knowing that I was becoming increasingly independent, and that they weren't going to change my mind about travelling alone.

I had always wanted to visit the south of India, but I was somewhat reluctant to travel alone. I talked to Ashok, my father's tenant, who had previously helped me get to Sawi. Ashok had known me for practically all my life, and looked upon me as a daughter, and when he learned of my wishes to visit the south, especially Bangalore, he called his sister-in-law, Vinita Bajaj, who was living there at the time, requesting that she take care of me.

Ravish Rastogi, a family friend in Delhi, took it upon himself to make all the arrangements as far as my flights were concerned. I caught the flight to Bangalore. Vinita had told me to look out for her, but never having met each other before, all we had to go on was the fact that I was wearing a green outfit, and she was wearing a beige outfit!

I received a very warm welcome in Bangalore. Vinita and her sons knew exactly what I had intended to do and had already planned my week. They showed me the most beautiful places around the south and I thoroughly enjoyed every second of it. I was loved, cared for, understood and accepted for what I was. That was exactly what I needed for my half-term. When I eventually returned to England, and to my course, my tutor said as soon as he saw me, "Somebody is happy and looking very relaxed." It did not need any explanation, it showed on my face. I will always be grateful to Vinita Bajaj and her family and, of course, Ashok, for that wonderful trip.

29

Doctor Sengupta

A week after my return, the family had planned a get-together at Dinki's house. Upon arriving, I found myself to be in extreme pain. My back was aching terribly, seizing as soon as I tried to sit down. In the grip of this seizure, I could neither sit, nor stand, and found myself lying on the floor, crying in pain. A doctor was called out, and he gave me a few painkillers, recommending that I seek further investigation for my back. I couldn't believe that the 'bruising' that I had in 1992 could be the cause of this pain, three years later.

The next morning, Manu took me to Newcastle Clinic to see a specialist. This doctor was well reputed for, shall I say, treating any complaints of pain with numbing injections. After he conducted the most painful examination he possibly could on my back, he offered me a cortisone injection, saying that I wouldn't feel any more pain. I knew by this stage that the problem with my back was more serious than any ligamentary injuries, which could have been cured by an injection, and thus rejected it.

Manu's reaction was somewhat predictable. He was furious on the way home, asking me whether I was a doctor, and if I knew so much about medicine, why did I even bother waking him up so early to go to the doctor, why didn't I self diagnose and sort my own problems out. I tried to explain my point of view, but Manu said that from then on, he wouldn't take me to any more doctors concerning this back pain. I was on my own for this. However, when I spoke to Sanju about my problems, she wanted me to follow my heart and to look up to the future and make the best of each situation. She never doubted my potential.

Some time passed, and Ms Davison referred Cathy Hayes to me, who was her helper and friend at the time. Cathy soon became just like Ms Davison for me, another amazing person who often took my burdens on her own shoulders.

One afternoon, Cathy jokingly said to me, "There must be someone on earth who can treat your back." I remembered Ravish Rastogi, our friend in India, and how his wife Madhu was treated by a Doctor Sengupta, who was and still is reputedly one of the topmost neurosurgeons. I felt sure that he wouldn't treat me, but thought it worth a try to call his office, and perhaps request a private appointment. Luckily, it was the good doctor himself who answered the phone, and on mentioning Madhu's name, he remembered that I had met him once when I went to visit her in his ward. Doctor Sengupta met me the next morning in Newcastle Nuffield Hospital.

I did not want anyone to know about this appointment, so I took a taxi and went on my own. I began by telling him that my rheumatologist thought that the problem with my spine was so complex that it was untreatable, that it would take a medical genius to sort my problems out, and even then, with the existing problems I had, if anything were to go wrong, I could end up in a wheelchair for life.

Doctor Sengupta smiled at me and asked me how I would feel if he could find that genius. Even at that time I had no idea what this person was capable of. I was merely here to ask for his advice, or for a recommendation. He told me to bend over, and I bent straight down and touched my toes. When he asked me to straighten up, I could not, and cried bitterly.

I was immediately sent for X-rays on my spine, but instead of having them standing upright, Doctor Sengupta had stated that I should have them when I was bent forwards, so that he could better see the problem.

I was also sent for a Magnetic Resonance Imaging (MRI) scan two days later, as I was told that Doctor Sengupta didn't want to miss anything that this scan may show him.

I had wanted to keep these appointments very much to myself, firstly because of what Manu had said to me, about not getting me treated himself, and secondly because, if Doctor Sengupta agreed that there was no problem in my spine, I didn't want anyone in the family making any remarks against me. However, Doctor Sengupta telephoned my house to discuss the results of both the MRI scan and the X-rays, a phone call which Ballu answered. Doctor Sengupta explained to Ballu and me over the speaker phone, in layman terms, that my spine was basically in two pieces, hanging on nerves. He said that I needed to see him urgently the next day, to discuss the procedures that I would have to undergo.

The next morning, after hearing this diagnosis, Manu took me to Doctor Sengupta's private clinic at his home. We were shown the scans, in which it could clearly be seen that two of my spinal discs were prolapsed, and that my spine was diseased with ankylosing spondylosis. The doctor said that he was surprised I was standing up, and running around the way I had been. I would have to have a major operation, because, as Doctor Sengupta said, simply falling over could be fatal for me.

The operation was a costly one, of course. Getting neurosurgery done through a private hospital is not a cheap way of being treated. Luckily, Manu had got health insurance for me through his company some months ago, and I was glad to have it.

Doctor Sengupta asked me when I was available for him to operate, as he knew I was still studying at the university.

I said to him that for my education, all I needed was my brain and my hands, and that he could operate on me as soon as he wanted. Thus, on the 12th of June, 1995, I was admitted to hospital, only a few months before the completion of my counselling degree.

I was given every detail of what was to be done to my spine. Doctor Sengupta would work with an orthopaedic surgeon, Doctor M. Gibson, to insert four metal rods and screws into my spine, to hold it together. I smiled, and told them to proceed with the operation, a reaction that aroused much curiosity in Doctor Sengupta, as he worried that upon hearing the intimate details of the operation, I may be swayed from having the operation altogether.

30
Dissectomy and Fusion

Mum and Dad had come to England a few days before I was admitted to hospital, not primarily to visit me, although they were my most welcome visitors at the time. They had come because Dad's health was deteriorating, and he also had to be admitted to hospital.

My back operation was called 'dissectomy and fusion of the spine, with rods and screws'. The operation lasted five hours and I lost five units of blood in that time. I had twenty-six staples in my back, to hold it together after it was cut open to allow them to operate. When I opened my eyes after the operation, I was covered in white sheets, with pipes hanging everywhere, not knowing whether I was dead or alive. I realised I was alive when I looked around and found my family there. I looked for Rohit but could not find him. I saw Manu. It was satisfying to know that he was there, and then I shut my eyes and could not remember any more for that day. All night I cried in pain. Nurses held me from both sides, making me comfortable, increasing the dose of morphine, giving me more medication. It was bad. They had given me morphine to ease the pain but I ended up with a rash all over my body, as I had an allergic reaction to this drug. I was most uncomfortable. My mind was a lot stronger than my spine. I thought, "Oh well, if I could survive the previous experiences, then I am sure I will survive this operation." When, in hindsight, I compare this operation to chemotherapy, I would most definitely say that the spinal operation was the most painful. The pain during my cancer treatment was different.

The hospital staff and my consultant made my stay in the hospital as comfortable as possible. From the day I had met Doctor Sengupta until after my operation, he was curious about my life. So one night he came at about ten in the evening, as usual, for his ward round, and ended up standing by the radiator for quite some time listening to my life story.

Although I felt very light as though a burden had been lifted after sharing the details of my life with him, somewhere deep down I felt very heavy. By now I knew one thing for sure, I did not want anyone's pity. Everyone in their own way knew that I had been unlucky, the understanding I was looking for was never there from any one of them. Maybe my expectations were too high. It was not a cold or a flu that everyone had and knew exactly how it felt. Ms Davison and Rohit saw me suffer in day-to-day life. Whenever I needed them, they were mostly available. The cancer group members, the university friends and tutors stayed in touch through writings, phone calls and visits to the hospital. Sadly, some people from my mum's family visited to merely show their pity to me, and to fulfil their social obligations.

Doctor Sengupta was one of the first people to hear my story with his full attention, and with an aim to help my situation. It was he who encouraged me to tell my life story, as in his view, I definitely had something to tell, something which others could benefit from.

Even if my family told me that I was very strong, I felt very weak inside. I knew deep down that it cost me a lot in feelings and heartache to be so strong. This, I could not express to anyone. It was so expensive to be alive. No one could ever imagine what I went through to carry on with my life at that time.

Usually, after each hospital treatment, I would make a point of treating myself to something, simply to lift my spirits. Most of the times I ended up in House of Fraser from where I'd buy a plain wool jumper. I had a pile of them, and wanted to do something to make them more attractive.

On my most uncomfortable nights in the hospital, I embroidered the jumpers to pin down my pain in beautiful patterns of flowers and leaves. When I looked at them during the day, I would look upon them as pain releasers, every thread being representative of the pain I felt. To everyone else they looked beautiful, but for me it was an exercise through the most painful of times. They still have a special meaning and always will.

I wrote meaningful words whenever I could. I searched for poetry, for sad words to match my moods. I had not sung for over ten years now, it was as if I had matured from that carefree child I once was, and the only songs that would come to mind when I wanted to sing, would be sad ones. I had lost all I was on the way here and was becoming a new person. I looked back to the person I had been – laughing, excited, singing at the drop of a hat. And suddenly, I saw myself propped on the pillow. I wondered who the real me was – the girl who did not know pain or the woman who had seen so much to the extent of being disillusioned. I started to discover who I was, attempting to get the best of the girl and combine it with the woman of wisdom who knew what life could be in either extreme.

It was time to go home after fourteen days in Doctor Sengupta's ward. I was determined not to put my heavy head on Rohit's shoulders. So, I told the doctor that I would only go home if he could arrange for a helper, which he did. I was offered the chance to be with Manu, but I thanked him, knowing I would be most comfortable in my own room, with my embroidered words, and near my little boy who was my strength.

Rohit had always seen me in pain. By this time, he understood me and my pain so well that he became one of the most considerate people in my life after my back operation. He was my very own nurse, always ready to help. He would touch me very gently as if I was the most beautiful and expensive flower in his garden, the very rare kind. He kept me going and did whatever I wanted him to do for me or for the house, cheerfully. He looked after me, although I had help from social services; from Ms Davison, and members of the cancer group, who visited me every week, cheering me up, and of course, from my family who, in spite of being busy with Dad's illness, helped me when they could. The satisfaction that they were all there was immense.

A counsellor, Mary B. Kelley, from my Hexham Cancer Group, came and spent one whole day with me. She talked about life and told me that I had experiences that one could not gain in a hundred years. People go through their lives and do not have the slightest clue of the kind of experiences that I had been through.

She told me that I was doing so well, crossing bridges of cultures, and knowing exactly what goes where, successfully combining and assimilating both Indian and English cultures. She felt that if I was only Indian I would not have been complete. It was very special talking to Mary, to learn her views about me, and to have her in my house.

Vera Bateman, a faith healer, came every Tuesday to heal my back, and to pray for me. Her healing was so good that each time she touched my back, I would fall asleep. I thanked God for these wonderful people from the cancer group.

On the one hand I was recovering from my back operation in bed, and on the other I was on the phone, interviewing people to complete my project for the counselling course. It was called "Indian Women and Counselling", a very interesting topic on Indian women's experiences: how they are treated, looked at, and what it means to be a single woman brought up in India but living in England. I finished my project, and sent it off by post to the university for evaluation. I passed. I was thrilled to receive my Certificate in Counselling. My family was very happy for me and my mother took us out for a meal to celebrate my achievement. It felt lovely. Rohit and I were very happy about our studies. In September 1995, Manu presented me a red Mercedes with a bouquet of flowers and his name as the numberplate. I thought he could not be with me all the time in person, so his namesake was parked outside for me to drive. He also sent a message saying, "No more falls from buses and public transport for you." I thanked him with my 'Wishes for Him' in poetry and he immediately had it framed and put it up in his lobby beneath a light that was always turned on, and jokingly assured me that he would always have money to pay for that light – all other bills would get second priority. Dad and I were feeling better, and I started to take my parents on long drives as Dad loved being in the country.

By this time I was walking around, or rather I was running around as much as I could. It was November 1995, my first winter after my back operation. I had a lot of stiffness and took extra painkillers in a vain attempt to numb what I was feeling.

The first six months after the back surgery was an active time for me: swimming, gentle back exercises and regular physiotherapy. I knew that if I did not do justice to this health regime, I would be in more pain, which I could not allow to happen, firstly for Rohit's sake, who could see my pain, even behind my false smiles, and secondly, for the running of my household, which was upside down without me.

31
An Escape

One day in 1996, I was sitting with Aunt Nirmal, talking about holidays, and my wish to take Rohit somewhere, as he hadn't been anywhere for quite a while. She promised me that if she made any plans, she would let me know and we would all go together. This promise materialised in April 1996, the Easter holidays, when Aunt Nirmal planned to take her two sons, Aman and Raman, along with Rohit and myself to Florida for two weeks.

Aunt Nirmal took upon herself all the arrangements for the trip. She had pre-booked our hotel, and hired a car in Florida, so she herself could plan our excursions. We visited Disney World, much to Rohit's delight. We also went to MGM and Universal Studios, the Kennedy Space Center and Busch Gardens. I don't actually know how we managed to visit so many places, considering that Aunt Nirmal had never driven a left-hand drive car, and didn't know any of the directions. Plus, the fact that she had four back seat drivers instructing her didn't really help, well ... not four, as Rohit did nothing but laugh at the rest of us.

Aman and Raman would be busy reading the maps, trying to work out where we were going, while the rest of us played *Antakshari*, an Indian game where one person sings a few lines of a song, and then the other has to sing a song beginning with the last letter of the preceding song.

Although my health did not permit me to go on any of the more exhilarating rides, it was very thrilling to watch Aman, Raman and Rohit enjoy them all. Aunt Nirmal gave me so much love and care, almost as if she was my mother. I felt I would always want to spend my future holidays with her. It was a beautiful experience.

Some people in society began to see me as a very strong person, especially after seeing Rohit and me so happy after all we had been through. Others pitied me for being so unlucky. I pitied them for thinking of me as unlucky. I received a lot of positive reinforcement for the things I was doing from my more immediate family, and I remember my mother's younger brother, Shyam Uncle, would always say that he liked to see me smiling and dressed properly. He loved to see me in a saree.

My family, my acquaintances and all those who cared for me, have always been an encouragement to me. There was a time in my life when I had wanted the respect of my husband, but now I had the respect of two men who were more important to me, my father and my son; times were taking a turn for the better.

My everyday health problems meant that I was always in a Catch 22 situation. If I had the medicine for arthritis then my asthma would flare up as a side-effect, if I didn't take the medicine however, I would be stiffer, resulting in more pain. My dream was to cope with my physical and mental problems and I strongly felt that further studies would be the best idea for the latter. I really wanted to be a counsellor psychologist, but I did not know how I would cope, having so little energy and not being able to work for long periods of time. I tried to understand what would be the right step for me, and at the same time I remembered my conversations with Dr Sengupta about the possibility of taking up writing as a hobby. His encouragement meant a lot to me. I had a mind full of thoughts and emotions but I simply did not know where to begin. My thoughts moved from further education in counselling, to writing.

Although I could not sit for very long at a time, I joined a part-time writing course at Newcastle University. Everyone knew that my back would not cope with all the straight sitting, so I would lie down sometimes during the sessions or keep two chairs to make myself comfortable. In the writing group at Newcastle University, my tutor, Gillian Allnutt, was very understanding; she knew why I was there. She knew I wanted to write about myself, but I couldn't look at my life from an outside perspective. Some of the members in that group loved what I wrote, especially Veda Kemper, but I felt I could not separate myself from my past enough to be able to write on different subjects and ideas. It was very hard but I got the certificate, "Writing from within", and was delighted to receive it.

I continued with the second and third parts of this course diligently. I remember one day, I woke up at seven in the morning to go to the university. I had completed the routine chores, sending Rohit to school with Ms Davison and taking a shower in a vain attempt to warm myself up, as it had been snowing all week. I was in two minds whether or not to attend classes that day, because the weather was so bad outside. At around ten, Mum rang my doorbell. She was staying at Ballu's house a few doors away and was looking for her trainers, which I had thrown out a few days ago without her knowledge. They were so ridiculously old that they were getting on my nerves, and I thought it was about time she had an incentive to get some new ones.

As I opened the door, I saw that the post had arrived. Placing it carelessly aside, I tended to Mum, telling her that I didn't know where her trainers were, and that she should perhaps get some new ones. She looked at me, knowing instantly that I had thrown them away, and sat in the lounge.

Whilst making her coffee that morning, I opened the post to find a letter from *Patchwork* magazine, telling me that a piece of work I had submitted had been published in one of their issues. I was ecstatic, euphoric and could not overcome my excitement as I shouted for Mum. She told me not to shout, as she knew that I had thrown away her trainers with other old shoes. I said yes, but I had just had my work published for the first time. I jumped up, picked up my bag and told Mum that I was going to the university to share the news with my writing class, with all those who knew exactly what it meant.

As I was getting in the car, she came running up to take a copy for herself. I looked at her, surprised, but felt wonderful to know that she had wanted it so badly that she ran barefoot to get it. As I was driving, I peeped into the future for the first time like a child sitting on his mother's lap, looking in the mirror, trying to recognise his face. The face, familiar, yet new, gave me a feeling that I had never experienced before. The child inside me felt new, bright, happy and content.

The following day I asked Mum if I should share my excitement with anyone. She was against it, and advised me to keep walking till I reached my destination, as my journey had just begun, and added that travelling gets challenging when one has an audience. I went over and over her marvellous description. I felt that it was good that only Mum knew about my work being published. I was frightened by thoughts of failure, and perhaps it was just as well that no one knew what I was trying to achieve. I knew my mum would never criticise me, no matter what. I felt the bond of closeness between us, and understood that it was something she herself was probably unaware of. She gave a special feeling that could make me do almost anything to see approval in her eyes. Her words and her wisdom to choose between right and wrong meant a lot to me.

By this time I was thinking that I had enough qualifications but I did not have the health to work or the ability to run my household like other people. There was a constant turmoil in my mind. Mentally, I wanted normality, to be energetic enough to fulfil my dreams and hopes, but unfortunately, I was not up to it physically – my body had other ideas. I wanted to make good use of my skills but I just did not know what I could do to earn a living, be useful to those in need of help and not be dependent on anybody. To sort that out, the arthritis care group and their magazine gave me the idea of joining another course in July 1997 – Personality Development.

32
Personal Development

I joined the course to find out if I could work for more extensive periods. The course was out of town in Bingley, and the ever-helpful Manu took me to attend S.T.E.P.S. (Steps to Excellence for Personal Success) by The Pacific Institute for five days. The organisers made me comfortable in the new environment and I met other young, disabled people who were fighting just like me, unable to accept certain realities of life that they couldn't control any more. They had to slow down. We all had to learn to slow down in life and have reasonable goals so that our bodies could cope better with our minds. I went through quite a lot of brainstorming throughout the course to find out exactly what strengths and weaknesses I possessed. Everything I wanted in life, had a price tag, which was a different level of physical suffering.

I understood that my body was too weak to keep pace with my dreams, and would not take any more pressure than I already had in bringing up Rohit and looking after my health needs. I was not fit enough to work every day, especially during winters, when the pain was severe. The side effects of medication, and my continual ill health, made me aware that with each passing year my health would deteriorate further. I could hardly think of a routine life as I was very susceptible to infections due to poor immunity. Health problems did not allow me to plan too far ahead. I lived one day at a time.

I was not well enough to sit and work throughout this course – I was the only one on the floor. While lying there, I realised that I could not be a counsellor psychologist because of my own health problems. Higher studies involved a lot of travelling, to and from the university, and my back could not cope with the pressure. I came back from this course accepting my health situation and my mental ability. I had no choice but to accept that my goal of becoming a counsellor was too high and I had been dragging my body around long enough without realising it. However, I continued thinking of how I could best utilise my skills. I also tried sending and receiving a lot of information on the exact nature of fibromyalgia, another illness that I had recently been diagnosed with.

The personal development course did me a lot of good. It helped me to accept the level of complexity of my health. I told the mentor of the course that I wanted to go around the world, I wanted to go away from my family and Rohit, to be able to sit down and write about myself, so that it may be helpful to those in need. On the way back from this course, Manu gave me a surprise by taking me to a live concert of Amitabh Bachchan, the famous Indian cine star. Manu had taken good care of me throughout our time together during this course. It was a nice way to end the journey.

It took me two years to find the strength to accept the fact that I was on my own, and to balance my physical and mental health and its capabilities. Rohit meant a lot to me, he was all I had, but he had to get on with his life and education, and I had to get on with mine. My family also meant a lot to me, but they had their own problems. I realised the need to get somewhere in life and stand on my own feet and tell the world that I had conquered defeat. Only I could make, shape or mould my own condition, environment and destiny. I completed ten years of being in remission from cancer, and maybe in the future, I should celebrate each added year as I do my birthday.

It happens to me every year, the weather, darkness and memories of the winter surface to remind me of the past as if

I have not moved on from where I was ten years ago. I struggle, plan and try to help myself but somehow end up where I don't want to be. I feel that a lot of things in life remain still and I cannot move them away.

One winter day I decided to do nothing and rest. Then the thought of trying to do something cropped up and made me uncomfortable. I built up my imaginary fears and tried to give in to the demands of my body. However, soon I was forced to choose between the stiffness of the body and the mind.

Suddenly it all changed when I saw Rohit's face. All my plans disappeared and I found myself moving from my previous still and stiff position. I got dressed, managed to walk slowly to the car and took him to the temple. He looked very happy. As soon as we saw the faces of people and connected ourselves to their spoken words, I was surprised to hear myself say that we were going out to enjoy ourselves tonight. Rohit looked at me, astonished at this unplanned outing.

I had no idea where the strength was coming from. I realised I was knotted, restless and still only in Rohit's absence. Everything changed when he was around. After praying in the temple and greeting people, I drove to the cinema.

It was a dark and cold night. I went into the cinema hall before him to find our seats, leaving him to bring popcorn and drinks. The movie was very entertaining and I felt a warming sensation after hearing his laughter. It was the best thing I had experienced all day.

When we reached home I was ready for bed although he looked wide awake, fresh and happy. He wanted me to stay up with him till midnight. I ignored him and, switching off the lights, said goodnight. At one minute to midnight, something fell out of the bedside cupboard. He sat up on the bed, and asked me to see what had made the noise. I turned the light on and there it was on the floor: a huge, heart-shaped red balloon that I was thinking of blowing up for him for the next afternoon. The words written on it were, "I love you enormously." I picked it up and showed it to him. He spread it out over the bed and read it aloud. He said, "I told you we should stay up till midnight, and it is your balloon that has woken us up to give me this message. What a perfect time to wish me Happy Birthday."

After a cup of tea, I thought of working on the computer. I wanted to find out where exactly my niece, Jo, lived in America, as she had now grown up and moved there for her studies. I turned on the computer. I opened up the encyclopaedia, and surprise, surprise, I had the wrong disk. I obviously did not know what to do and I tried looking for my work files. I felt angry at not finding them and shouted for Rohit. He told me to move so he could see what was wrong. He took hold of the mouse and moved it around. "It is all here, Mum," he said. I heaved a sigh of relief and looked at his face, that face which was teasing me for not knowing enough about the computer. He was right, I thought. I thanked God and him for having found my precious files.

During the personal development course in 1997, I had been given a schedule book, and tapes to follow a practical day-to-day routine, to relax, eat with my son, laugh, and take each day's challenges as they came. It taught me to rest when I was tired and be away from people and situations that confused my mind and body, especially those people who kept watching me constantly, waiting for me to fall. When I learnt to say that I was okay, people kept reminding me of the life I had had. The two books, *Your Erroneous Zones* and *I'm OK, You're OK* helped me tremendously towards positive thinking. I recommend them to anyone going through a difficult time in life.

Rohit was eleven years old. He had a mobile phone, and was attending the Royal Grammar Senior School, confident of travelling on the Metro from home to school. He was growing up fast. At the same time, he built his first computer for Ballu to prove that he could do it. Ms Davison had driven him in her car everywhere so far but now she could see that he was a very capable boy, both of us could see that. I could never thank Ms Davison enough, as she had taken care of him better than I could have hoped to, in the years preceding this one. I remembered how she would wake up every morning, even in the coldest of winters, to take Rohit to school. Sometimes, real mothers fail to do that for their own children.

My world became smaller. I only socialised with people I felt comfortable with and those who understood my situation in life and accepted me for what I was. I continued with the 'Writing from Within' course at Newcastle University, once a week. I also did short courses on flower-making, decoupage, ribbon embroidery and continued swimming on my better days. I kept myself busy most of the time, if nothing else, by just listening to music, or baking something. I forgot my physical discomforts for the short periods of time when I was able to do something or the other. It became a habit.

On March 25th, 1999, Chandni gave birth to her third child, a baby boy, Hitesh, affectionately known to us all as Manav. A great social pressure was lifted from Ballu's shoulders with the birth of a son. I remember driving in the early hours of the morning to Hexham Hospital with Rohit to see Chandni and her baby boy. Chandni smiled at Rohit, telling him that he would always be her first son.

In January 2000, I took my parents and my son for a pilgrimage in India. In having my son and father, I had the universe with me. We had a wonderful time. I felt honoured to be able to travel along with them. Our trip started in Delhi, and ended at Vaishnodevi, a hilltop shrine. It was my first holiday with my parents and son together. My parents loved every bit of it.

Rohit kept travelling everywhere on his school trips. I never let him miss an opportunity to go where he could, as I wasn't able to take him myself. He simply loved it. Planning a journey became a habit.

163

33
India Revisited, Twice

I started to have health problems again due to fibroids and a large cyst in my ovary, and an incontinence problem that had existed since Rohit's birth. I was putting on weight as I was taking more medicine to control the problem and it was hurting my back more than before. My doctor suggested further investigations and the answer was hysterectomy and colposuspension operation. To make sure that the cyst was not cancerous, I had the operation. It did not feel strange as by now I was comfortable being in and out of hospitals. Filling in familiar health forms and packing bags with my favourite reading material to stay in hospital was nothing new for me, it was like a holiday from home.

It became crucial to lose weight and keep active. Although I tried my best, I was much slower than before. My family, son and friends kept me going. Another hard winter meant another trip back home to India. Rohit and I set off, but and due to bad weather, the flights got delayed and we were in Paris for a day till the next flight to Delhi.

Air France had arranged for all the passengers to stay in a beautiful hotel just outside of Paris. Rohit spent most of his time downstairs, in the lounge, whilst I lay upstairs in bed. He told me he was going to reception to get a phone card, and after a while, I went looking for him, worried that he had got lost.

Upon finding him, he asked me if I had locked the room upstairs, to which I replied that I had. He then asked me to come outside the hotel for a minute, and pulled me onto the bus that was picking up passengers for the airport. I was astonished, not knowing what he was doing, telling him that we weren't supposed to leave the hotel in case they called for our flight. Besides, all my money and valuables were in the hotel room. He insisted I stay quiet, as he needed some information from Paris Airport, and assured me that we would be on the next bus back.

As we arrived at the airport, he left me standing quite a way behind him, and exchanged the sixty pounds he had, of his own money, for what were French francs at the time. He returned with two tickets for the train that left from the station in the airport. He told me that the train was quicker to get back to the hotel, and so, reluctantly, I agreed. Deep down, I was worried that I didn't speak a word of French, and as far as the family knew, I was on a plane to Delhi.

A while later, we had to change trains. I enquired why, but Rohit wouldn't tell me anything, scaring me more than ever, as it seemed as though we were headed into the city, instead of the hotel on the outskirts.

We arrived at a train station, the name escapes me. By this time, I was getting angry, asking Rohit where he had taken me. Rohit was calm and happy, as though he had arrived where he wanted to be. Taking out a map, he told me that I would see where were in a few minutes.

Surely enough, a few minutes later, we were standing at the bottom of the Eiffel Tower, and in no time, he had bought tickets, and we were at the top. He bought a disposable camera, and although the photographs didn't come out clearly at all, the memory remains vivid in my mind. I realised then that Rohit had a strong will of his own, even at the age of thirteen, and I saw how much faith I had in him, letting him lead me blindly to where he wanted me to go.

Safety is important, but taking risks in life are just as important. We concluded our trip with a stay in a five-star hotel in Delhi and arrived home, smiling, from Delhi to Newcastle. Rohit had a black suit, tailored for him in India, and he insisted on wearing it home. As I waited for my ride home, I realised how far we had come. 'God gives and forgets, we take and forget.

In January 2002, I again came to India and took my son and parents to famous and favourite places in the south, from Bangalore to Kanyakumari. Dad sang the most romantic songs of the famous Indian singer Mohammed Rafi every day, and I took hundreds of happy photos of us all. It felt great to have managed to live and enjoy life. The same year, back in England, I volunteered to counsel people in need, through cancer groups and the Indian community, feeling that people in a similar situation, who could not afford to hire a counsellor, could come to me. I received a few thank you cards every year at Christmas and I loved them because they were my achievements. I learnt that when my body was not hurting so much, I could do physical activities and during a bad patch of cold weather and physical illness, I could mentally keep myself busy by reading, writing, praying and talking to people over the phone, listening to their problems and mirroring their thoughts back to them to help them find their own answers. Gradually, the more I became useful to those who needed me, the more comfortable and at peace I felt.

Time rolled on beautifully. I began smiling again as I saw my achievements mount up before me. I recommenced my studies, and was accepted to begin a Masters Degree in Counselling at Durham University in 2002. The year before, Rohit had attained his first diploma from a Correspondence School in computer programming, quite an achievement at the age of fourteen. He began his second diploma in the repair and upgrading of computers. Doing a full-time course in the winter for long hours was tiring, but instead of fatigue at the end of the day, I was overjoyed that I was managing to move around more.

About the same time, Manu presented Mum and Dad with the most beautiful house in Ludhiana. He had exported everything except the bricks to have that home specially built for his parents, an extravagant show of his affection.

Taking vacations with Rohit was always a welcome release, and when the opportunity came to visit Canada, to spend some time with Doctor Marcus, a wonderful psychiatrist who had often helped me through some difficult times, I took it without a second thought. We spent a few days in Calgary, with Doctor Marcus and his family, before travelling to Banff, via a helicopter ride around the Rocky Mountains in Canmore.

Banff was perfect, and from there we went to Lake Louise, which was quite honestly one of the most amazing places both of us have visited. Rohit hired a rowing boat and rowed me to the end of the lake and back. Our trip ended with a visit to the Niagara Falls, lunch at the Skylon Tower, a look at Edmonton Mall, then back to Toronto, and back home after our visit to the CN tower.

I realised that happiness is a butterfly. When you run after it, you never manage to catch it and one day suddenly it lands on your shoulder.

By now, I had memberships to some of the best institutions, dedicated to making the lives of the less fortunate, better. I became a member of the Northern Cancer Network Panel, The National Health Service Health Improvement and Modernisation Panel, and the Rotary Club. I involved myself heavily in fund-raising for a project in Calcutta to open a neurosurgery centre for the underprivileged.

34
My Father

My dad was a loud, slow-moving and happy-go-lucky person. But in times of worry he changed into the most punctual and alert person, working hard to remove any obstacles out of his way, and never resting till the tasks he undertook were completed. He achieved great success and happiness and was always proud of his plans and thinking. He had to be sure of everything as he never took risks. In business, he always weighed his pros and cons. His gentle heart would weep easily to see even a stranger in pain. He liked works of charity, and would often plan visits so he could feed birds and animals. His aim in life was to have a good time, always, and to make the most of what he had. He never settled for anything less than perfect for himself or his loved ones. At times he needed a push due to physical and psychological constraints, but most of the time he encouraged everyone's efforts and success. Faith in God kept this person going through the ups and downs of life. He usually saw a bright side in every situation. He was never jealous or unfaithful towards anyone. His anger frightened everyone but me. I just smile as I think of him.

On the 18th of March 2004, at 1.30 a.m., I received a call from Manu. In the background, I could hear crying. His words poured from my ears to my heart, breaking the rhythm of my heartbeat and bringing life to a halt. 'Dad is no more.' I put the phone down and sank, still not believing that what

I heard was true. How could just eight hours of time make that much of a difference? I had spoken to Mum on the phone that day. I dialled Mum's number, telling her, 'I'ɪɪ coming, Mum.' Life cancelled all of my appointments for that day, and maybe beyond.

The family assembled in Manu's lounge, as he handed out roles for the family to undertake during this period, keeping as cool a head as he could. He told the family that none of the children would be accompanying him to India, as it would be too traumatic a scene for them to witness. Rohit was told to stay at home, with Tuli. Much to my pleasure, Rohit spoke against this, saying, "If I have a choice, I'd like to go." I'm glad that Manu respected this wish almost in an instant, saying, "What's the point in all of us working so hard, if we can't respect our children's wishes?"

I flew to India at 5 a.m. with Manu, Ballu, Rohit and Sanju. I could still hear Dad's last words, just eight days ago, when I had returned from India to England: "Don't come without Rohit to India. He needs you. I don't like it when he is not here with you. Go home and be happy with Rohit. God knows what is in store for me as I am not feeling well." Rohit lost a father today. Dad was the only father he ever had. Although Rohit was vulnerable and the family wanted to protect him, he had made his choice and was grateful to everyone for letting him have a last glance at Dad's body.

As William Shakespeare says, "The voice of one's parents is the voice of God for to their children they are heavens' lieutenants." We lost one of our heavens' lieutenants today. My head will always remember his hand over it, my heart will always remember his blessings for me.

The next day, we arrived home at 6 a.m. Mum in a white suit, teary-eyed and with a broken heart, ran barefoot to the front gate of the house. It felt strange to be the parent to my mother. I held on to her, and she just slipped into my arms. Everyone helped her and took her in. She had turned so very pale and frail. I wished I could turn back the clock, snatch

Dad back and tell life, "He's mine", but all I could do was feel helpless. We waited for Dinky's arrival. All of us went to the morgue to see my dad's body; it was cold and we spoke no words, yet I could hear him say that all of us had never failed him for anything in life. We all had loved, cared and looked after him to the best of our abilities. I heard him say that his time had arrived. He had lived, laughed, cried, eaten the best, worn the finest and died without a care. He did not trouble anyone in his end. He wasn't hurt. He did not cry. He did not speak. Death is silent. He was God's and God took him in his embrace.

We drove back from the mortuary. Lots of people came to console us. It was difficult to say whether time rolled by or lay still. Mum kept talking of him, remembering him all the time. She was all alone now, in a mansion empty without him.

On the 20th, people came from different towns. The newspaper carried the details of his final journey with his photograph. Everyone talked about him and consoled us. The atmosphere, with servants serving water to all, was heavy with his memory. I was here just last week. When I flew, I left a very precious package of mine, my parents in the house. I left a man in the bedroom, my dad. On my return, the package was not the same. My dad was gone. I felt robbed and cheated. We all waited patiently till Dinky arrived, sobbing her heart out as the truck from the mortuary brought her dead father's clay-like body home. It seemed as if he had been waiting to show his face to her, just like he had always waited for her on the other side of death. I cried out, "Daddy don't go alone! I want to go with my Daddy. I love you, Daddy," yet he spoke no word.

I saw the male members of my family bravely bring his body into the house for his last bath. Manu, Ballu, Rohit, Munimji and Dad's friend, Rammurthy Uncle, gave him a bath. They wrapped him in a towel I had embroidered for him in red, blue, yellow, green and purple threads, on a thick

170

white bath sheet, reading "Rishidev". I had presented it to my dad on his birthday some years ago. He wanted to keep it safe and clean. I could tell it was precious to him. I never knew he would be wiped with it for this purpose. My heart tore inside me as I realised it. Mum wanted to dress him in a dinner suit, but the stiffness of the body would not allow that. She gave his little necessities, the best clothing, best after shave, his handkerchief, just like she always did whenever he went anywhere. His body came out in the front garden wrapped in white, lying on a handmade ladder tied with ropes. Hundreds of people awaited him. Families paid their last tributes and performed the Hindu rituals. Everyone touched his feet, but I kissed his cheek, although I could not shake his hand the way we used to each time we met or departed. This time his hands were tied by the travesty of destiny. I placed my 10-year-old niece Nidhi's letter on his chest. It was time for my father's clay to depart from the luxuries of his beautiful home, from his loving family and his beloved wife Shiela, whom he fondly called 'Sheel'.

The whole family was followed by a huge crowd of mourners, chanting 'Ram naam satya hai' (God's name is the ultimate truth). The Mercedes he loved carried the ladies he loved the most, while the male members of the family who loved him immensely accompanied him on his last journey in the truck.

We braved our way into the crematorium, each step weighing heavier than the previous one. Further rituals were performed by Manu, the eldest son. While Manu was brave, the rest of us broke down when we saw alley no. 4, a modest cemented platform covered with red bricks that was to be his last bed. The yard was full of all sorts of wooden chunks – huge, heavy, light, thick and thin. Some men laid down the body and covered it with piles of wood, reading mantras while the sons lit the pyre. I stood watching the dust, flames and the sunshine. The trees stood silently. It seemed as if the wind stood still and the birds too became silent. In the background, chanting of prayers continued as the flames grew higher and higher. We were told to leave, with my mother leading the way ahead of everyone, leaving the flames to burn my father's clay-like body. My feet refused to move yet someone held me and moved me along with Mum to stand at the front gate of the crematorium. We held our hands together and thanked the procession of hundreds of people who were leaving. We said thanks to all. At the end, we left the flames on the pyre to do their job.

I felt that my father's soul and his love was with all of us. He has gone to the celestial kingdom, in a better place where there is no pain, no sieving of stones out of a plate full of the lentils of life. My father's soul is resting in peace. We all have the satisfaction of having done our best for him. His love is his reminder. I am grateful to God and proud to have been a part of his life. I must take care of myself and my son, and live as he advised me to live, being closer to God than to humans beings, loving Rohit, doing my duty in life.

The king of the house is gone but his queen, Mum, is here in his place. She has taken over his role to fulfil his aspirations. I shall take care of all that he has left – my family, the same blood running through all our veins. I shall love them as much as I can, to be close to the one man I loved the most, my daddy. After my father's passing away, in the darkest hour of our lives, we saw sunshine. Manu, after a lot of struggle, was able to bring back a part of Sawi's existence to soothe our still-fresh wound. After fifteen years of waiting, lovely Anu and pretty Vanu walked into our home. Embracing them, we felt Sawi in our arms again. In my overwhelmed mum's eyes, happiness trickled down, wetting her already throbbing heart and longing soul. All of us thanked God.

November came, and Rohit's 18th birthday, upon which there was a quiet celebration. Neither he, nor I wished to have any festivities that day, as dad's passing was too raw a

172

memory. Until this day, Rohit had been known legally as Rohit Sood, as his father, even at his own request, had not granted permission for Rohit to change his name to Malhotra. Rohit said to me, "I don't want to keep the name of a man who couldn't take time out of his life to see his son." After his 18th birthday, when he was legally allowed to change his name without anyone's consent, he changed it to Rohit Rishi Dev Malhotra, much to my pleasure, in honour of the only father he ever knew.

35
Unshackled Me

It is January and I am in India by myself. It looks so different now, maybe times have changed, maybe I've changed. I remember running through those very streets all those years ago, without a care in the world, knowing that I was safe and secure, and I remember being happy then, always smiling. My eyes rake along the floor, looking down, sighing at the knowledge that now, even a simple smile can trigger a pain that makes smiling a lost cause. The very air that I grew up breathing, seems to choke me, corroding my very essence. I slip away from the window, sliding back into bed, my dressing gown tossed carelessly to the floor as the coolness of the sheets engulfs my body once more. I close my eyes in the knowledge that this day will be the same as all of those that have come before it. I feel a sense of worthlessness creep around me like a very discomforting chill seeming to emanate from everything I look at. I remember those cool winter mornings, the first time I was taken from this town. I remember the day I left for England, and the promise of better times, the promise of prosperity. The look on my father's face as I left him, knowing I would be away indefinitely, still sends a chill down my spine. The look on my brother's face, as I walked through the desolate airport terminal, reminds me of the fear of uncertainty that was always present, the fear that crept through me, wondering when I would see those streets of my childhood again.

I pull the blanket up over me, sighing as these memories float through my mind. I try hard to remember everything, just as it was, but my mind seems like a tape that's been played too many times, and starts to crackle and fade away. My eyes close once more, my thoughts trail hopelessly, trying to grasp something with the slightest hint of solidarity in it, something I can cling onto to save me from the downward spiral that seems to be my life. I see my son, that everlasting presence that seems to bring focus to my life, and remind me of what it was to hold onto hope, and look forward to good times.

My eyes flutter open, the light switch clicking sharply, as my tea is placed by my bedside. I exchange the usual pleasantries with the helper, listening to the monotonous sound of sandals pattering along the marble floor as she leaves, letting darkness creep in once more. There is no one here apart from a couple of house-helpers, who cook and clean and look after me.

I am sitting here recording all of my thoughts on cassette tape, so that one day it may be heard by those who really need to hear it. I have learnt a lot in the years I've had; a lot of things have happened. I look at society differently now. I used to care deeply before about what others might think. I had a fear of tradition, different cultures, society and others living around me. In the past I always managed to hide my pain and tried to walk around wearing a mask, so that I did not bother others.

Now I have come to a point in life where I am open, where I am able to talk about my pain. I am not frightened to tell anybody that I need a walking stick. At times, I cannot walk without help. If someone is walking with me they have to know that I may need their hand to hold, to be able to keep going. I have differentiated between being strong in mind and weak in body. My mind is not fractured any more. It is one healed piece and in peace. Physical and verbal abuse have built a lot of inner strength and determination in me and have made me fearless.

I do not need to hide my physical illness. I have been ill but that illness has made me mentally stronger. Although my experiences in life have chipped away parts of my being, it meant I was carving my own shape, which I did not realise until now. Whatever I am mentally today, it is all because of my experiences. I have come a long way in my mind to understand the meaning of life. It does not matter what sort of physical pain I have. The best way to forget pain is to fill the mind with positive thoughts.

The history of women has been the history of silence and I would like to revolt against this silence.

My courage and conscience cannot stay still when I see other girls suffering. Female education is the only remedy that can root out evils like the dowry system and gender discrimination from our society. It will enable women to grab their destinies in their own hands. They must stand up for justice and self-respect in matters of life. Education is the only eye opener for our society's younger generation.

After having braved all the tortures inflicted on me I believe that it is not the activity of the evil but the inactivity of the virtuous that destroys our society. One must stand up for self pride and justice always.

I've experienced too much too soon in my short married life and in the course of my life, I have met all three kinds of people – people who have immediately turned up their sleeves to come to my help, people who have turned up their noses as they did not want my miseries to cast a reflection on themselves or the future of their children, and those who have not turned up at all. I would like to follow the type who turned up their sleeves to help me out of my sufferings.

I think from here on my road trifurcates. The first goal is to I invest my time and energy in people and contribute all my might in fighting the system and changing it. Secondly, I should raise my goal a few notches every time and achieve it. It will give me the satisfaction of achievement and happiness. The third is to forgive and forget and become spiritually enlightened. I have taken guidance from our scriptures and learnt forgiveness from the sandalwood tree. It leaves fragrance on the very axe that hews it down. The more you rub it on the stone, the more perfume it emits. When burnt, it wafts its essence in the entire neighbourhood. This is the enchanting beauty of forgiveness in life.

Due to my own self-knowledge, I forgive all those people in my life who may have intentionally or unintentionally hurt me. If it wasn't for all of my experiences with these people, I would not be the person I am today. Thus, I thank them for their contributions in helping me grow, heal, and learn to let go. They have helped me to discover my own strengths, moulding me into a sharing, spiritual and creative person, with a feeling of the purest freedom.

A person is made up of a mind and a body. If the physical pain is extreme, you have to fine tune the mind to create a balance. You need to bring the mind up to a level at which you forget your physical troubles, by keeping yourself occupied and by learning to relax. You need to help yourself, need to turn your thoughts away from the physical pain. It is difficult. Sometimes little things disturb this balance, but you should try to blot them out. Only you know the pain, where it is, how sharp it is, and what the remedy is. Remember that if you are alive, there is an answer to everything, there is a cure for everything. You're lucky.

Fly as high as you can, walk as far as you can and be known for living amongst other people. You are a part of this world. There is a star in the sky with your name written on it. It is shining and it is yours, only yours. You are not living by any accident. God wants you to live and you are very special.

By saying all this to you, my friend, I have claimed my star, achieved my goal and announced to everyone that I am alive. It is a new start, a new road, and I am waiting to see the junctions, the roundabouts and the destination I shall eventually reach.

A sigh escapes my lips, the tears wiped from my face as Prerna ends her story. The pen is out of ink, there is nothing more to write. Life is put into perspective in an instant. There is no more room for hatred and anger, poisons that once plagued my mind. My soul is liberated, as I hope yours is.

About the Author

Born in India, Amita Malhotra's childhood experienced the soil of Punjab and the spirit of traditional Hindu culture. She did her schooling in Ludhiana and moved to England. There she met Prerna, whose experience of an arranged marriage with an Indian settled in England gave her a sharpened perspective on the non-resident Indian community – their loneliness and conflicting values. This added a new dimension to her understanding of life and found expression in her writing. She has been living in Great Britain for the last twenty-two years.

Author's Other Publications

Published by the National Disability Arts Forum in Shelf Life, edited by Katie O'reilly, forworded by Nabil Shaban, designed by Dave Everitt, printed by A1 WhizzPrint, Gateshead.

Death

I work day and night every ticking minute, constantly taking life from all ages, races, colours, religions, sizes and shapes of human beings. I see no difference between rich, poor, dark, light, young, ill, healthy, strong, weak, gentle, cruel or other types.

I have a duty to end the life of that which is ever born. No one lives forever is my message and I keep on reminding everyone every day. I can give signals as I go rushing and snatching. My work involves going anywhere and anytime. People find me dark, horrible, frightening and a threat. I'm seen as a blessing in some places and violence in others. I take away pain and the suffering of the ill and give relief to their bodies. I make space by taking the old. I free humans from the everyday tortures of work, fights, violence and fears. I take the person and leave a silent message for their loved ones to remember their life. I make people mourn so they can understand the meaning of laughter. I remind them to be happy as long as they are alive. I force people to get as much as they can before I knock on their doors.

I check people's patience when they are ill. If they are strong-willed and happy to fight the disease, the pain and stiffness, I can leave them to limp a little longer. What I do to the people left behind sometimes can be agonizing and unbearable.

People who get attached to their loved ones cannot let them go. I give them a chance to learn to let go and find more meaningful ways of living.

I am the ultimate truth - I have some meaning to all. I see people come into the world empty-handed then get attached to materials, relationships and hold on to power and property. People come empty-handed and they go empty-handed. People at birth and death may differ. They come crying but leave silent.

Life attaches-death takes it apart. Life is pain - death is ease.

Death is silent, still and unchangeable. It cannot be bought, sold or exchanged. It has various ways and reasons for coming. It feels smooth like silk after a long rough journey of life. It smells like a rose after the stinking experiences of being born. It gives the person a chance to freshen up after years of living one day thousands of times. It sounds like music after life's loud, disturbing, meaningless voices. In life people take many drugs, alcohol and pain-easing medicine but death takes all pains away forever and leaves the body in healing peace. It doesn't hurt or harm the person in any way. It only marks the body: Life to finish and soul to be free.

It can have many effects on people who go through seeing a death of a loved one. It follows them and takes away their peace of mind and leaves them to moan 'til they die. A mother finds it the most difficult to see her own child's death. It burns her heart and leaves scars and emotional disturbance 'til her own death.

Although death is the same, the way it comes to people has different effects. At times it is seen as punishment, an accident, or carelessness; it is horrible, traumatic, violent.

181

No amount of human power can conquer death, it cannot be changed, beaten or won, if it is there, it exists, and lasts forever. It quietens down the human first cry, to the last spoken word. It is the end of a journey (life can speak, death has no voice, life can move, death is still).

Silence Within

In the mirror-wired of water

The silence within, when the sense of the earth unites with the sense of your body

Why should it mean

So much that at least one person has seen the Inside of your life -

Dissolved into a trembling shimmer on the surface of the wave?

God is silent

When the last friends have fallen asleep

Give me the rejoicing rhythm of my seasons

Think of the flowers they never have to spin or weave

My eyelids close in peaceful hope

Whoever you may be, you invented me

When words are choked, their meaning becomes clear. I go beyond death to awaken life

I invite the clouds to dance my ballet

There are times when I enjoy whistling in the darkness

I make people feel alive, since I put their strength to the test If man is a pilgrim, why should he stick to the earth? Tears are too precious, too dear to afford.

Enclosed into an all too narrow space

You sweep men away like a dream.

Death is a presence that walks the road of life with me

Death gnaws at my belonging in the world

Death will be no stranger, it will not rob me of the life I've had

What is real, what I love, belongs to me, no one can take it away from me.

I am not afraid to meet myself, yet I am afraid to meet myself.

In the light of dawn, it is not a snake lying in the corner, but an old rope.

When you can name your fear, it begins to shrink

No one can say with certainty what is going to happen tonight, tomorrow or next week.

Time can bring anything to the door of your life

There will be an evening, a morning or a night, when I will have to make the journey from this life.

When I go, there will be an empty place at the table.

— **Amita Malhotra**